Good Eating's

Barbecue!

Great ideas for
backyard get-togethers

by
Heather McPherson

The Orlando Sentinel

This book is for Vernell ``Red'' Birden:
A barbecue master with more fire and spirit
in her soul than any person I know.

You can't stoke a barbecue fire like this without some help. Thanks to these fine folks who helped make it possible:

Orlando Sentinel Editor John Haile, Deputy Managing Editor Steve Doyle, Lifestyle Editor Mick Lochridge and Sentinel copy editors April Medina and Susan Whigham.

John Blexrud, Colleen Dykes, Lita Geier and Cindy King of the Sentinel's Marketing department.

Art director Melissa Huerta and illustrator Lisa Frasier who made everything look so swell.

Sentinel recipe testers Betty Boza and Phyllis Gray. Sentinel photographers Tom Burton and Roberto Gonzalez.

Polly Golden of the Florida Beef Council, Marlys Bielunski of the National Cattleman's Beef Association, Anita Fial of Lewis & Neale, the National Pork Producers Council, American Dairy Association, American Spice Trade Association, Bacardi, Catfish Institute, Florida Watermelon Board, Florida Tomato Committee, G & R Farms, National Honey Board, National Potato Board, Meat Board Test Kitchen, Nestle Toll House Kitchens, North American Blueberry Council. Quaker Oats, Bean Education & Awareness Network, California Table Grape Commission, Progresso, Food From Spain, Mushroom Council, Land O' Lakes and North Carolina Sweet Potato Commission.

And, several participants in Good Eating's annual Great Florida Barbecue Sauce Search Sauce: Debbie Bass, Manuel Bolanos, John G. Chanin, Steve Chappell, Edythe Dombrowsky, Tom Dorman, Donna McGregor Fant, Bob Gest, Kim Hughes, David Isreal, Amy Jackson, Julius Johnson III, Blanche Johnston, John L. Kalajian, Dorothy Kingsbury, Chiko Lampitt, Gertrude Madden, David Mesnekoff, Ed Muurahainen, Nikki Norman, Richard Ousey, Dan Parma, Enrique W. Perez, Craig Pergrem, Margaret Rogers, Marian R. Rowen, Angelo V. Sano, Dorothy Sayre, James Skelly, Karen Sullivan, Bonnie L. Tidmore, Tim Turner, Carmen Vega, Carl Walters, Judy Wick and Donna Zegler.

And last but not least — The Grand Island Sunday Night Barbecue Brigade: Jake Vest, who likes to light the fire; Laurie Vest, who keeps the white wine chilled; my husband, Spencer Pettit, who makes sure everything is cooked to perfection, and Mady Whalen, who graciously puts up with all of us.

McPherson, Heather
    Barbecue! Great ideas for backyard get-togethers /
Heather McPherson

    ISBN 0-8092-2773-8

            Library of Congress Cataloging-In-Publication Data
McPherson, Heather
    Barbecue! : great ideas for backyard get-togethers / by Heather
McPherson.
            p.   cm.
        Includes index.
        ISBN 0-8092-2773-8 (alk. paper)
        1. Barbecue cookery. I. Title.
    TX840.B3M447 1998
    641.5'784--dc21   98-22523
                                                                        CIP

CONTENTS

A Party With a Plan

Getting sauced . . .

Whether you like yours with a pinch of pucker or a hefty hit of heat, barbecue sauces can spark debate around the backyard grill as fast as a match takes to a mound of instant-light charcoal.

To set the tone of their sauces, some folks insist on a hefty pour of white cider vinegar, while others prefer a courageous mix of Scotch bonnet, datil or jalapeno peppers. Many sauce makers prefer a generous glop of molasses for sweetness and color. But the most creative cooks look deeper into their cupboards or refrigerators to add simple and subtle flavor twists.

From mashed mangoes or apricot marmalade for sticky sweetness to a cup of strong black coffee or bourbon for a bold jolt of character, the ingredients in some of the sauce recipes in Chapter 1 combine to create flavorful sauces worthy of any cookout.

So why go to all this trouble to make a sauce when supermarkets sell a bajillion fine and dandy commercial brands?

You do it because, let's face it, the thrill of your friends saying "oh-my-gawd, I've died and gone to heaven" about your homemade sauce and exclaiming that you are to barbecue what Elvis was to blue suede shoes is a lot more gratifying than unscrewing a plastic cap and breaking a paper safety seal with a steak knife.

Besides, "fine and dandy" is the culinary-school equivalent of a passing grade. Who wants fine and dandy when you can have blue-ribbon worthy homemade sauce to slather on chicken or ribs?

And before you start making excuses, consider these points:

If you think it's too expensive to make your own sauce, think again.

Barbecue sauce ingredients are generally inexpensive.

If you think it takes too much time to make your own sauce, think again. The most labor-intensive aspect of preparing sauce is chopping, but then that's why God gave us food processors and blenders, isn't it?

Even if you aren't from the from-scratch school of cooking, the speed-scratch alternative can produce delicious results. Simply doctor up a bottled sauce with fresh ingredients (rosemary, garlic) or exotic items (balsamic vinegar, imported dark beers), and you have gone from just fine and dandy to the gold medal platform in no time.

I suggest you leave the convenience food category to the folks who make products like Easy Cheese and keep barbecue sauces right where they belong — simmering real slow in deep pots in home kitchens.

I hope you enjoy the sauce recipes in the next chapter, and I encourage you to be adventurous when making them. After all, subtracting a fresh ingredient here and adding another interesting tidbit there will help you add your own russet-tinged thumbprint on a backyard feast.

Setting the stage . . .

The scent of citronella is in the air. The tiki torches are lined up around the patio. And in the distance the old Waring is whirling up a batch of creamy pina coladas.

Get out the Jimmy Buffett tapes: The party is moving outdoors.

You don't need a yard that looks like a botanical garden or a pool fashioned after the swimming hole at some fancy hotel to throw a festive bash.

When it comes down to it, outdoor parties aren't much different than indoor parties except for two things: The tableware should be unbreakable, and lighting adjustments have to be made after sunset.

Unbreakable tableware just seems to get better and better. And discount party stores have brought the home cook items once available only to caterers. Many are crafted so well that you can't tell if they are acrylic until you pick them up. These are priced from less than a dollar to about $25. Because they are reusable, it's money well-spent.

When setting tables, remember the great outdoors offers a pretty busy canvas, so keep things simple. For example, use coordinating solid-colored plates with stemware on a neutral straw table covering.

Reusable serving pieces are sold open stock (that is singly, not in sets) giving you more freedom to mix bold colors in a place setting. For example, a lime green salad bowl can be paired with a cool blue dinner plate. Dessert can ride high in purple-stemmed margarita-style glasses.

Discount and import stores are great sources of interesting lanterns, torches and outdoor candles. Remember to have them in place and ready to light before the sun sets.

With the table set and the nuances of lighting dealt with, I say let's have another round of pina coladas. Your blender or mine?

Barbecue basics . . .

Marinades and rubs add unique flavors to meat for the grill. A marinade is a highly seasoned liquid used to impart flavor, and, in some cases, tenderize tougher cuts of meat. A rub is a highly concentrated blend of herbs and spices that flavors the exterior of the meat as it grills.

Marinades . . .

Marinades consist of liquid ingredients such as fruit or vegetable juices, wine, water and oil in combination with seasonings and herbs. Meat soaks in the marinade mixture for several hours or as long as overnight to soak up flavor and-or to be tenderized. To tenderize, a marinade must contain an acidic ingredient such as lemon juice, wine, vinegar or yogurt; the acid penetrates meat fibers to help tenderize them.

How to marinate . . .

Always marinate in the refrigerator; never at room temperature.

Allow 1/4 to 1/2 cup of marinade for each 1 to 2 pounds of meat.

Marinades may be cooked or uncooked. Cooked marinades should be completely cooled before adding to meat.

The tenderizing effect of a marinade is usually about 1/4 inch from the cut surface of the meat.

A heavy-duty plastic food bag is convenient for marinating; a glass utility dish may also be used. Select containers in which the meat will fit snugly but lie flat.

Turn meat occasionally during marinating so that all sides are equally exposed to the marinade.

For tenderizing to take place, most meat cuts must be marinated at least 6 hours, or as long as overnight. Marinating longer than 24 hours causes the meat fibers on the surface to break down, resulting in a mushy texture.

For flavor, marinate 15 minutes or as long as 2 hours.

Marinades may also be brushed on during grilling. Reserve a portion of the marinade to use for brushing before marinating the meat. Marinades that have a high sugar content or contain other ingredients that might burn easily should be brushed on only during the last 20 minutes of grilling.

Reserved marinade may also be served as a sauce with the grilled meat.

Discard used marinades; never reuse marinades.

Rubs

Rubs are applied to the surface of the meat just before grilling; they need no standing time. However, for convenience, rubs may be applied several hours in advance; the coated meat should be refrigerated until grilling time. Flavors become more pronounced the longer the rub is on the meat. You can create your own blend of seasonings for rubs or use a commercial blend.

How many briquettes?

To estimate the number of briquettes you need, spread them in a single layer, extending about an inch beyond the food you're going to cook.

On windy and humid days, or when you're cooking larger pieces of meat that take longer to cook, you may need to add more charcoal.

Consider the kinds and brands of briquettes you're using. Natural charcoal burns hotter and longer and creates less ash than charcoal briquettes.

Lighting the fire

Pile the briquettes in a pyramid in the center of the firebox. For standard briquettes, drizzle liquid lighter or fluid over the entire charcoal surface. Wait for one minute, then ignite with a match. (Never use gasoline or kerosene to start charcoal.)

Arranging the coals

After lighting the fire, leave the briquettes in a pyramid until they look ash-gray by day or glow red after dark. Self-lighting briquettes will need to burn about five to 10 minutes before they're ready. Standard briquettes will need to burn for 20 to 30 minutes.

Once the coals are ready, spread them out for either direct or indirect cooking. The method of cooking you choose will depend on the type of food you're cooking.

How to cook

Direct cooking: This method is a fast way to cook smaller cuts that you normally would broil, such as steaks, chops, patties, or fish fillets. Use long-handled tongs to spread out the hot coals in a single layer. For even heat during cooking, arrange the hot coals about a half-inch apart. This also will help reduce flare-ups caused by fat dripping from the meat onto the coals. You'll grill the food directly over the coals, but take care not to cook it too quickly or char the outside.

Indirect cooking: Follow this method when you have a roast, ribs, whole birds, or other large cuts that you usually would roast. You also can grill smaller cuts without worrying about flare-ups and charring, although they will take a few minutes longer. Place a disposable foil drip pan in the center of the firebox. Then, using long-handled tongs, arrange the hot coals in a circle around the pan. You'll cook the food over the drip pan with the grill covered.

Judging fire hotness: Be sure to check the recommended cooking temperature in the recipe before putting the food on the grill. Just like cooking on a stove, not all foods grill at the same temperature.

You can determine the cooking temperature of the coals by holding your hand, palm side down, above the coals at the height your food will be cooked. Then start counting the seconds, "one thousand one, one thousand two." If you need to withdraw your hand after two seconds, the coals are hot; after three seconds, they're medium-hot; after four seconds, they're medium; after five seconds, they're medium-slow; and after six seconds, they're slow.

Adjusting the temperature: When the coals are too hot, raise the grill rack and spread the coals apart. Close the air vents halfway and remove some of the hot briquettes.

When the coals are too cool, tap the ashes off the burning coals with tongs. Move the coals closer together and add more briquettes. Lower the grill rack and open the vents to allow more air to circulate. Adjust gas or electric burners to a higher setting.

Grilling tips for pork

Pork back ribs, also called baby back ribs, are cut from the blade and center section of the loin and are known for the "finger meat" between the rib bones. Back ribs are a favorite because they are meaty and easy to handle. Plan 1 pound per person when purchasing pork back ribs, which generally weigh between 1 1/2 and 1 3/4 pounds per rack. **Spareribs**, which come from the belly or side of the hog, are the least meaty of all pork ribs, but they spare nothing in taste. Plan on 1 pound per serving. Both back ribs and spareribs are the preferred ribs for restaurants. The meatiest of ribs are **country-style**. Cut from the rib end of the loin, these pork ribs offer more meat than bone and can be eaten with knife and fork. A half-pound of country-style ribs satisfies most appetites.

Grill ribs over indirect heat by banking medium-hot coals around edges of a covered grill (or bank coals on one side of the grill), or roast in a 350 F oven. Grill or roast ribs for 1 1/2 hours to 2 hours. Longer cooking renders ribs more tender. The ribs are done when the meat wiggles from the bone.

Grilling tips for fish and shellfish

● Shrimp can be peeled before or after they're grilled. Peeled shrimp require constant basting to keep them from becoming tough and dry. To prepare shrimp with the peels, snip off the legs and cut the shells down the back and the belly. Leave shells attached and use the skewers to keep them in place.
● Remove grill from heat source and liberally spray with non stick coating.
● Thick fish fillets and steaks grilled over medium heat require about five to seven minutes per side.
● Wrap delicate fish with seasonings in parchment, foil or even wet corn husks.
● Basting yields moist results when grilling salmon, grouper, swordfish or shellfish.
● Scallops are best skewered and cooked over medium-low coals.

Grilling tips for turkey

- Select a turkey or turkey breast that will fit comfortably on your grill with the lid on.
- Defrost the turkey or turkey breast completely before cooking. Always defrost in the refrigerator, not at room temperature, which can allow dangerous bacteria to grow.
- Remove the neck and giblets from the cavity if cooking a whole turkey. Remove the backbone and break the wishbone, if cooking a turkey breast.
- Rinse a whole turkey inside and out. Rinse both sides of a turkey breast in cool running water. Pat dry with paper towels.
- Season bird inside and out with your choice of herbs or spices. Do not stuff; bake stuffing separately.
- Grill covered over low heat if using a gas grill; if using a charcoal grill, cook over coals that are gray ash outside and glowing red inside. Replenish the coals with fresh briquettes when the fire burns low, or about once an hour.
- Baste every 10 minutes with garlic-flavored olive oil or plain olive oil.
- Close the grill cover when not basting the turkey or turkey breast.
- Add water-soaked wood chips to the coals if desired during the last 30 to 45 minutes of cooking to impart a distinct wood-smoke flavor.
- Cook the turkey or turkey breast until a meat thermometer inserted in the breast registers 170F to 175F. Total cooking time should equal about 14 to 15 minutes per pound.
- Allow the turkey to rest at room temperature for 15 to 20 minutes before carving.

Grilling tips for beef

Steaks such as sirloin and filet take well to grilling, as do flank and skirt. Rub unmarinated steaks lightly with vegetable or olive oil and cook directly over the coals. If a steak is thicker than 1 1/4 inches, fatty, or coated with an oily marinade, consider cooking it over indirect heat with the cover on.

Here's a guide to cooking beef steaks medium-rare to medium on the grill:

Times are approximate for meat directly form the refrigerator, put on a grill heated with medium coals.

- Rib-eye: 3/4 inch, 6 to 8 minutes; 1 inch, 11 to 14 minutes; 1 1/2 inches, 17 to 22 minutes (grill covered).
- Rib steak (small end): 3/4 inch, 6 to 8minutes; 1 inch, 9 to 12minutes; 1 1/2 inches, 22 to 27 minutes (grill covered).
- Porterhouse/T-bone: 3/4 inch, 10 to 12 minutes; 1 inch, 14 to 16 minutes; 1 1/2 inches, 20 to 24 minutes (grill covered).
- Top Sirloin, boneless: 3/4 inch, 13 to 16 minutes; 1 inch, 17 to 21 minutes; 1 1/2 inches, 22 to 26 minutes (grill covered); 2 inches, 28 to 33 minutes (grill covered).
- Tenderloin: 1 inch, 13 to 15 minutes; 1 1/2 inches, 14 to 16 minutes (grill covered).
- Flank, marinated: 1 1/2 to 2 pound, 17 to 21 minutes.
- Top round, marinated (recommended cooking to medium rare (145 F): 3/4 inch, 8 to 9 minutes; 1 inch, 16 to 18 minutes; 1 1/2 inches, 25 to 28 minutes (grill covered).
- Chuck shoulder, boneless, marinated: 3/4 inch, 14 to 17 minutes; 1 inch, 16 to 20 minutes.
- Chuck top blade, boneless: 1 inch, 18 to 22 minutes.
- Ground patties (cook to 160 F or until centers are no longer pink): 4 ounce, 11 to 13 minutes; 6 ounce, 13 to 15 minutes.

Sensational Sauces

MILD SAUCE

HOT SAUCE

Amy Jackson's Hot 'n Spicy BBQ Sauce

Yield: 6 cups

1 (28-ounce) bottle ketchup
1 cup honey
1/2 cup Dijon mustard
1/2 cup vinegar
2 tablespoons Worcestershire sauce
2 tablespoons grape jelly
2 tablespoons light brown sugar
3 small cloves garlic, crushed
1 teaspoon cayenne pepper
1 teaspoon chili powder
1/4 teaspoon black pepper
1/8 teaspoon ground ginger

1. Combine all ingredients in a large saucepan. Heat on low until grape jelly has completely dissolved.

Note: Great with hamburgers, ribs and chicken wings.

Margaret Roger's Juicy Barbecue Sauce

Yield: 1 1/2 gallons

1 (24 ounce) bottle ketchup
1 pound dark brown sugar
1/2 tablespoon prepared mustard
1 tablespoon black pepper
1/2 cup (4 ounces) onion juice
3/4 cup (6 ounces) Florida orange juice
3/4 cup (6 ounces) pineapple juice
3/4 cup (6 ounces) mango juice
4 tablespoons corn starch

1. Combine all ingredients in a 1 gallon plastic or glass container. Mix well.
2. Pour into a Dutch oven or kettle
3. Cook over low heat until mixture begins to thicken. If too thin add more cornstarch. When cool pour into squeeze bottles with large hole in tip.

Notes: This is enough sauce for 10 pounds of chicken. Baste ribs over the grill and turn frequently, using squeeze bottle to keep moist.

Edythe Dombrowky's Peppy Barbeque Sauce

Yield: 6 pints

1 (28-ounce) bottle ketchup
1 (14-ounce) bottle chili sauce
1/3 cup prepared mustard
1 tablespoon dry mustard
1 1/2 cup firmly packed brown sugar
1 (5-ounce) bottle Pickapeppa Sauce
1 1/2 cups red-wine vinegar
1 cup fresh lemon juice
Dash of Tabasco sauce, or to taste
1/4 cup Worcestershire sauce
1 tablespoon soy sauce
1 tablespoon salad oil
1 (12-ounce) can beer

1. Combine all the ingredients listed and mix well.
2. Store mixture in the refrigerator for several weeks, or freeze indefinitely.

Notes: For use on oven barbecued meats, no previous cooking needed. For use on grilled foods, simmer sauce 45 minutes until thickened, if desired.

Manuel Bolaños' LemonQ

Yield: about 2 cups

1 (15-ounce) can tomato puree
1/2 cup lemon juice
1/2 cup natural honey
3 cloves garlic, finely chopped
1/2 medium onion, finely chopped
1 tablespoon corn oil margarine
1 teaspoon paprika
1 teaspoon chili powder
1/2 teaspoon ground cumin
1/2 teaspoon ground oregano

1. Combine the tomato puree, lemon juice and honey in a saucepan. Cover and cook on low heat, stirring occasionally.
2. In a separate skillet on low heat, melt the margarine and saute the garlic and onion.
3. Stir in the spices. Remove from heat and pour into tomato mixture. Continue cooking sauce, covered on low heat, for approximately 3 hours.

Marion R. Rowen's Jamaican Barbecue Sauce

Yield: 3 cups

1 cup cider vinegar
1/4 cup lemon juice
1 tablespoon Worcestershire sauce
1/4 cup brown sugar
1 tablespoon prepared mustard
1/2 teaspoon salt
1 cup ketchup
1 cup tomato sauce
1 small onion, minced
1/4 teaspoon cayenne pepper

Combine all ingredients in a saucepan. Bring to a boil. Reduce heat and simmer for 30 minutes.

Debbie Bass' Famous Barbecue Sauce

Yield: 1 1/2 quarts

1 (32-ounce) bottle ketchup
1 (14-ounce) bottle chili sauce
1 cup Galliano liqueur
4 tablespoons Worcestershire sauce
1 cup dark brown sugar, packed
1/2 cup lemon juice
1 (16-ounce) can cranberry sauce
with berries
or 2 cups homemade cranberry sauce

Mix all the ingredients well. Cook over low heat for approximately 10 minutes. Do not boil. Cool and baste on chicken, ribs or seafood.

Notes: To make your own cranberry sauce to use in this recipe, combine 2 cups sugar with 2 cups water in a large saucepan. Heat to boiling and cook for 5 minutes. Add 1 pound fresh or frozen cranberries. Cook until the skins pop, about 5 minutes. Remove from heat and stir 2 cups into barbecue recipe.

Blanche Johnston's Blushing Barbecue Sauce

Yield: 2 1/2 cups

1 (16-ounce) can cranberry sauce
1/2 cup sugar
1 1/2 teaspoons curry powder
1 teaspoon cardamom
1/4 teaspoon ground ginger
1 teaspoon onion salt
1/2 cup malt vinegar or wine vinegar
2 tablespoons dark corn syrup or
  molasses
1 1/2 teaspoons picante sauce

In a 2 1/2 quart saucepan, combine all ingredients. Heat to boiling, reduce heat and simmer for 5 minutes. Remove from heat and beat with a rotary beater or a whisk until thoroughly blended.

Note: This sauce is a dark, pretty color as well as palatable. This is easy and economical to make yet has a lot of zing and zest.

Chiko Lampitt's Barbecue Sauce

Yield: 3/4 cup

3 tablespoons crunchy peanut butter
1 teaspoon coriander powder
1/2 cup kecap manis (sweet,
  Indonesian soy sauce)
1 1/2 tablespoons vegetable oil
2 tablespoons ketchup

Mix all ingredients until well-blended. Use as a marinade or a basting sauce.

Note: Kecap manis is a soy sauce sweetened with palm sugar. It is available at Oriental markets.

John G. Chanin's Florida Citrus Barbecue Sauce

Yield: 2 cups

4 tablespoons unsalted butter
4 green onions with tops, chopped
1/4 cup cider vinegar
1/4 cup olive oil
1/2 cup fresh orange juice
3 cloves garlic, crushed
2 tablespoons soy sauce
4 tablespoons dry sherry
1/4 teaspoon freshly ground black pepper
2/3 cup light brown sugar, packed
1 teaspoon dry mustard
1/2 cup ketchup
1/2 teaspoon ground ginger
1/4 teaspoon crushed red pepper flakes
1/4 teaspoon hot Hungarian paprika
Grated zest and peel from
1/2 fresh orange
Grated zest and peel from 1/2 fresh lemon

1. Melt the butter in heavy, 2-quart saucepan over medium-low heat. Add the green onions and cook until soft, about 10 minutes. Stir occasionally to keep the onions from browning. Remove the pan from heat.

2. Add all remaining ingredients and whisk gently to combine.

3. Return the mixture to heat and bring to a boil, stirring to prevent sticking.

4. Reduce heat to low and simmer partially covered for 20 to 25 minutes. Remove from heat and cool to room temperature. Strain the sauce.

Notes: John G. Chanin, creator of this recipe, suggests marinating chicken pieces in the cooled sauce for up to 6 hours in the refrigerator. This sauce can also be used as a baste for smoked chicken. Baste the birds every 10 minutes during the final 30 minutes of smoking.

Carmen Vega's BBQ Sauce Home Recipe

Yield: 2 cups

1 small can tomato sauce
1 small can stewed tomatoes
1/4 cup Worcestershire sauce
1/2 teaspoon soy sauce
1/3 cup duck sauce
2 tablespoons Dijon mustard
1/4 teapoon freshly squeezed lime juice

1. Drain the stewed tomatoes, reserving the juice, and chop the tomatoes in very small pieces.

2. Mix the tomatoes, reserved juice and tomato sauce.

3. Combine Worcestershire sauce, soy sauce, duck sauce and Dijon mustard and stir into tomato mixture. Add the lime juice and stir to blend well.

4. Refrigerate for at least 1 hour before using.

Bob Gest's What About Bob? Barbecue Sauce

Yield: 1 quart

1 (32-ounce) bottle ketchup
8 ounces apple butter
8 ounces vinegar
1/2 teaspoon hot red pepper or a
dash of hot sauce
1/8 to 1/4 teaspoon ground cloves
1/8 to 1/4 teaspoon cinnamon
1/4 to 1/2 teasppon crushed garlic
1/4 teaspoon salt
1/4 teaspoon black pepper
1/4 teaspoon paprika
1 bay leaf

Mix all ingredients well and refrigerate overnight.

*Note: The creator of this sauce encourages any-
one who makes it to experiment with the spices,
the amount of apple butter and other ingredients.
He also said a dash of liquid smoke adds a nice
flavor.*

John L. Kalajian's Barbecue Sauce

Yield: 1 quart

2 tablespoons butter
1 onion, chopped
1 green bell pepper, chopped
4 cloves garlic, crushed
3/4 cup cider vinegar
1/4 cup fresh lemon juice
1/4 cup brown sugar
1 cup chili sauce
2 cups ketchup
2 teaspoons Worcestershire sauce

1 teaspoon dry mustard
1/2 teaspoon hot pepper sauce
1 bay leaf
2 sprigs parsley
12 black peppercorns, whole

Heat the butter in a large saucepan. Saute the
onion, pepper and garlic until the onions are slightly brown.
Add the rest of the ingredients. Bring to a boil,
reduce the heat and simmer for 1 hour. Strain to
remove solids.

Tim Turner's Hickory Cognac BBQ Sauce

Yield: About 6 1/2 cups

1 (20-ounce) bottle ketchup
3 ounces hickory-flavored liquid smoke
3 ounces lemon juice
3 ounces molasses
1 1/2 cups water
1 cup vinegar
1 1/2 large Vidalia onions, chopped
4 cloves garlic, minced
2 jalapeno peppers, seeded,
deveined and finely chopped

1 1/2 tablespoons seasoning salt
1 1/2 tablespoons black pepper
1 teaspoon cinnamon
1 1/2 cups light brown sugar
2 ounces Hennessy Cognac

1. Combine ketchup, liquid smoke, lemon juice, molasses, water and vinegar. Heat to a low boil.
2. In a blender, process onions, garlic, jalapenos. Add to ketchup mixture. Add salt, pepper, cinnamon, brown sugar. Simmer, covered, for 2 hours, stirring occasionally. Remove from heat. Let mixture cool; add Cognac.

Tom Dorman's Barbecue Sauce

This recipe won The Orlando Sentinel's 1997 Great Florida Barbecue Sauce Search.
Yield: 7 cups

1 (32-ounce) bottle Heinz ketchup
1 cup water
2 tablespoons olive oil
1/2 cup prepared mustard
1/4 cup Grandma's molasses
1/8 cup honey
1/8 cup light brown sugar
3 tablespoons apple cider vinegar
1 teaspoon salt
1 teaspoon black pepper
1 teaspoon garlic powder
1 tablespoon Creole seasoning

1 tablespoon Old Bay seasoning
1 tablespoon chili powder
2 tablespoons mesquite barbecue seasoning
2 tablespoons mesquite smoke marinade
Juice from 2 lemons
4 tablespoons Worcestershire sauce
1 tablespoon lemon-pepper seasoning

Combine all ingredients in a large saucepan. Heat and stir until ingredients are well-blended and heated through, about 15 minutes.

James Skelly's Chinese-Style BBQ Sauce

Yield: about 2 1/2 cups

1 cup finely chopped onion
2 minced garlic cloves
1/2 stick butter
5 ounces tomato puree
1/2 cup brown sugar
1/3 cup soy sauce
1/3 cup rice vinegar
3/4 teaspoon chili powder
1 ounce honey

1. Combine all ingredients in a saucepan. Let ingredients cook down over medium heat for about 30 minutes, stirring occasionally.

Notes: "After boiling baby backs ribs, spread the sauce over the ribs and brown under a broiler on both sides," says sauce creator James Skelly.

Nikki Norman's Now This Little Piggy Was Barbecue Sauce

Yield: about 3 quarts

3 cups tomato sauce
3 cups tomato ketchup
1/2 cup liquid smoke
2 cups white vinegar
1 medium onion, grated
3 large cloves garlic, minced
1 tablespoon chili powder
1 cup pineapple preserves
1 cup guava jelly
1/2 cup prepared horseradish
1 tablespoon Tabasco
3 tablespoons prepared mustard
1 cup light brown sugar
2 bay leaves

1. In a large pot or Dutch oven, combine all ingredients. Bring mixture to a rolling boil over high heat, stirring frequently to prevent the onions, garlic and pineapple preserves from scorching.
2. Reduce heat to low and simmer for 1 to 1 1/2 hours, stirring occasionally. Remove from heat and cool to room temperature.
3. Remove bay leaves. Cover and refrigerate until ready to use.

Note: "This is an excellent sauce to use for basting pork ribs and chicken. Serve additional sauce for dipping with barbecued meats," says Nikki Norman.

Carl Walters' Classic Barbecue Sauce

Yield: 6 cups

Seasoning mix:

1 1/2 teaspoons black pepper
1 teaspoon salt
1 teaspoon onion powder
1 teaspoon garlic powder
1/2 teaspoon white pepper
1/2 teaspoon cayenne pepper

Main ingredients:

1/2 pound bacon, minced
1 1/2 cups chopped onion
2 cups beef or chicken stock
1 1/2 cups bottled chili sauce
1 cup honey
3/4 cup dry roasted pecans, chopped
5 tablespoons fresh orange juice
Rind and pulp from 1/2 orange
2 tablespoons fresh lemon juice
Rind and pulp from 1/4 lemon
2 tablespoons minced garlic
1 tablespoon Tabasco
4 tablespoons unsalted butter

1. Combine the seasoning mix ingredients in a small bowl and set aside.

2. In a pot or 2-quart saucepan, fry the bacon over high heat until crisp. Stir in the onions, cover pan and continue to cook until the onions are dark brown, about 8-10 minutes, stirring occasionally. Stir in the seasoning mix and let cook for about 1 minute.

3. Add the stock, chili sauce, honey, pecans, orange and lemon juices, orange and lemon rinds and pulp, garlic and Tabasco. Stir well. Reduce heat to low and let cook 10 minutes more, stirring frequently.

4. Remove orange and lemon rinds. Continue cooking and stirring for 15 minutes. Add the butter and stir until melted.

5. Remove pan from heat. Let mixture cool about 30 minutes. Pour mixture in the work bowl of food processor or blender and process until pecans and bacon are finely chopped. (Depending on the size of your appliance, you may need to do this in batches.)

Note: "This recipe is a classic. It is reminiscent of the old South when people took the time to do things right and used fresh ingredients," says Carl Walters. He uses the sauce on chicken, pork and ribs.

Steve Chappell and David Mesnekoff's Irresistable Hot Sauce

Yield: 1 quart

11 datil peppers, or 2 Scotch bonnets, or 10-16 jalapenos, finely minced
1/2 cup brown sugar
1 (28-ounce) bottle ketchup
1/4 teaspoon allspice
1 to 2 teaspoons yellow mustard
3 cloves garlic, finely minced
1/2 teaspoon olive oil
4 to 5 teaspoon vinegar
1/2 teaspoon Worcestershire sauce
2 tablespoons freshly squeezed lemon juice
4 ounces crushed pineapple, or 1/2 cup mango with juice from a jar (mash mango), or 1/2 cup mashed peaches and juice, or 1/2 cup apples and apple juice, or 4 ounces Mott's cinnamon apple sauce

1. Combine all ingredients in a large pot. Bring mixture to a boil, stirring occasionally as temperature rises. Reduce heat to low and let simmer for 1 hour.

Note: David Mesnekoff says that this concoction can be used as a barbecue sauce or as an all-purpose condiment. "As you try it, you find the heat gently grows on you. It is truly irresistible."

Gertrude Madden's Sweet & Tangy BBQ Sauce

Yield: 3 cups

1 large bottle of Russian dressing
1 package Lipton Onion Soup Mix
1 medium-size jar apricot preserves

1. Combine all ingredients in a saucepan. Heat and stir until ingredients are well-blended and heated through.

Note: Gertrude Madden suggests coating any meat with this sauce during the last five minutes of barbecuing. Also, she says, "use any leftover sauce for dip."

David Isreal's Canton BBQ Sauce

Yield: about 4 cups

1 large shallot, minced (3 to 4 tablespoons)
1 1/2 tablespoons olive oil
1 cup ketchup
1/2 cup hoisin sauce
1/2 cup apple cider vinegar
1 teaspoon cayenne pepper
1 cup water, divided
1 cup beer
4 tablespoons dark brown sugar
4 teaspoons Dijon mustard

1. In a saucepan over medium heat, combine shallots and olive oil. Saute, but do not allow to brown, about 3 minutes.

2. In a bowl, combine ketchup, hoisin sauce, apple cider vinegar, cayenne pepper, 1/2 cup water and beer. Blend ingredients thoroughly and add to saucepan.

3. After the mixture warms up a bit, add the dark brown sugar, stirring until completely dissolved. Reduce heat and let mixture simmer for 15 minutes. As the mixture reduces in volume, gradually add the remaining water until mixture reaches the desired consistency. Remove pan from heat and stir in the Dijon mustard. Let sauce rest for at least 1 hour before using.

Note: David Isreal says that this concoction "works well for both grilling and smoking." Also, Isreal suggests letting the sauce rest for six hours or more for best flavor. For the beer, he recommends using "regular stuff — like Budweiser — not light, microbrewed" beer.

Angelo Sano's Stick-to-Your-Ribs Sauce

Yield: 6 cups

1 cup strong black coffee
1 cup Worcestershire sauce
1 cup Heinz ketchup
1/2 cup cider vinegar
1/2 cup brown sugar
3 tablespoons chili powder
2 cups chopped Vidalia onions
1/4 cup minced hot chili peppers
(use less for a milder sauce)
6 cloves garlic, minced

1. Combine all ingredients in a saucepan. Simmer and stir mixture for 25 minutes.

2. Remove pan from heat and chill slightly. Puree the sauce in a blender or food processor until smooth. Store in refrigerator.

Donna McGregor Fant's Rita's Recipe for Renaldo's Return

Yield: about 4 cups

1/2 cup chopped onion
2 tablespoons butter or margarine
1 clove garlic, minced
1 cup ketchup
3 tablespoons apple cider vinegar
3 tablespoons brown sugar
1 (8-ounce) can crushed pineapple, undrained
1 jar Gerber Baby Mango dessert or 1/2 cup chopped fresh mango
1/2 teaspoon salt
1/2 teaspoon pepper
1 tablespoon chili powder, more or less to taste
1 jalapeno pepper, seeded, deveined, chopped (optional)

1. In a saucepan, saute onion in butter until transparent. Add garlic and saute briefly being careful not to brown.

2. Add the remaining ingredients and simmer, uncovered, for 20 minutes.

3. For a chunky sauce, use as is. For a smooth sauce, carefully blend in the work bowl of a food processor or blender until smooth.

Note: This recipe's unusual name comes from the short story that was attached to the recipe. Fant wrote about a Caribbean woman named Rita, whose spouse, Renaldo, becomes smitten by another woman until Rita woos him back with her special barbecue sauce. Donna McGregor Fant, who is a country songwriter, suggests basting chicken ("or meat of choice") with this sauce during the last 15 minutes of grilling.

Craig Pergrem's Premium Sauce

Yeild: 3 cups.

1/2 cup tarragon vinegar
2 tablespoons Worcestershire sauce
1 medium onion, quartered
2 teaspoons crushed garlic
2 teaspoons chili powder
1 (32 ounce) bottle ketchup
3/4 cup sugar
1/4 cup hot sauce (preferably Durkee)

1. Place vinegar, Worcestershire sauce and onion in a blender or food processor. Blend until smooth.

2. Add sugar, garlic and chili powder and blend again.

3. Pour ketchup into a medium saucepan and add the blended mixture. Simmer 30 minutes. Add hot sauce and simmer 1 hour longer.

Kim Hughes' Hukilau Sauce

Yield: 1 cup

1/2 cup ketchup
2 tablespoons soy sauce or tamari
1 tablespoon oyster sauce
1 tablespoon honey
1 tablespoon rice wine vinegar
2 teaspoons Asian sesame oil
1 tablespoon grated fresh ginger
2 cloves garlic minced
1/2 teaspoon five-spice powder
1/2 teaspoon monosodium glutamate (optional)

1. Combine all ingredients and use as a marinade. Brush on meat, chicken, fish or other seafood while grilling.
   Makes 1 cup.

Note: Kim Hughes adapted this recipe from one given to her by her Hawaiian sister-in-law, Winnifred Crosby Flick. Hughes recommends placing a pork tenderloin in a resealable plastic bag and and covering it with the sauce. She allows it to marinate all day in the refrigerator and roasts it at night. She has also used the sauce with stir-fried pea pods.

Bonnie L. Tidmore's Basic Barbecue Sauce

Yield: 3 cups

3/4 cup brown sugar
1 1/2 tablespoons dry mustard
2 teaspoons salt
1/4 teaspoon black pepper
1 teaspoon ginger
1 (8-ounce) can tomato sauce
1 cup Florida orange juice
2 tablespoons minced onion
2 cloves garlic, minced
3 tablespoons parsley
2 tablespoons Worcestershire sauce

1. Combine all the ingredients in a large bowl.
2. Marinate meat in sauce for 1 hour before cooking. Baste meat frequently with sauce while cooking. (Discard sauce after using as a marinade.)

Note: This recipe yields enough sauce for 5 pounds of pork spareribs. It's also great on chicken.

Julius Johnson III's Aunt Lettie's Barbecue Sauce

Yield: 1 quart

1 cup chopped onion
3 cloves garlic, crushed
3 tablespoons olive oil
1 (28-ounce) can tomato puree
1/4 cup lemon juice
2 tablespoons Worcestershire sauce
1/2 cup molasses
1 teaspoon dry mustard
1 teaspoon thyme
1 teaspoon oregano
3 tablespoons brown sugar
1 teaspoon salt

1. In a large saucepan, saute the onion and garlic in the olive oil until tender.

2. Add the tomato puree and remaining ingredients. Simmer for at least 15 minutes.

Judy Wick's Peachy Chinese Barbecue Sauce

Yield: about 2 cups.

1/2 cup chopped onion
2 cloves garlic, crushed
2 tablespoons Asian sesame oil
1 (12-ounce) jar peach or apricot preserves
1/4 cup ketchup-based chili sauce
1/3 cup red-wine vinegar
1 teaspoon hickory salt or table salt
2 teaspoons soy sauce

1. Saute the onion and garlic in oil in a small saucepan until tender.

2. Stir in the preserves, chili sauce, vinegar, hickory salt and soy sauce.

3. Simmer for 20 minutes. Serve with chicken or pork.

Donna Zegler's Grand Citrus Chocolate BBQ

The chocolate adds a subtle touch of richness to this wonderful sauce.
Yield: about 2 quarts

1 (20-ounce) bottle Heinz ketchup
1 teaspoon cornstarch
3 1/2 teaspoons molasses
1 teaspoon Coleman's dry mustard
1 teaspoon Worcestershire sauce
1/2 medium-size Vidalia onion, finely chopped
1/3 cup apple cider vinegar
3 dried whole habanero (Scotch bonnet) peppers, chopped
1/2 teaspoon mace
1/2 teaspoon cayenne pepper
1/2 teaspoon adobo
1/2 cup firmly packed brown sugar
1/4 cup light corn syrup
1/4 cup Ghiradelli semisweet chocolate chips

Zest from 1 orange (see note)
1/4 cup Grand Marnier

1. In a large saucepan or pot with a lid, combine ketchup, cornstarch, molasses, dry mustard, Worcestershire, onion, apple cider vinegar, habanero peppers, mace, cayenne pepper, adobo, brown sugar and corn syrup. Stir until well-mixed. Heat over medium-low for about 20 minutes.
2. Lower heat to low. Add chocolate chips, orange zest and Grand Marnier to mixture. Cook for 15 minutes.

Note: Zest is the minced colored peel of citrus. Use a potato peeler or zester to remove just the outer layer of skin — do not use the white pith. Donna Zegler recommends her sauce on pork ribs.

Dorothy Kingsbury's Barbecue Sauce

Yield: 1 pint.

Juice of 1 lemon
1/2 cup water
1/2 cup ketchup
1/4 cup butter
1/4 cup vinegar
1 teaspoon ground red pepper
Dash of black pepper
1 teaspoon salt
2 teaspoons Worcestershire sauce
4 cloves garlic, minced

2 medium bay leaves
4 teaspoons liquid smoke
1/2 teaspoon thyme leaves, crushed
1/2 teaspoon rosemary leaves, crushed
1/4 teaspoon turmeric
1 teaspoon sugar

1. Combine all ingredients in a large stainless steel or enamel saucepan.
2. Simmer for 15 to 20 minutes.

Ed Muurahainen's T-Bone Eddie's Florida Fire Ant Barbecue Sauce

Yield: Makes 5 1/2 cups.

1 (32-ounce) bottle ketchup (preferably Heinz)
1 (8-ounce) jar Grey Poupon mustard
1 cup packed brown sugar
1/4 cup Worcestershire sauce
2 tablespoons dry sherry (not cooking sherry)
6 tablespoons seasoned rice vinegar
2 teaspoons Lawry's seasoned salt
2 teaspoons garlic powder
4 teaspoons mild chili powder
1 teaspoon cumin
2 tablespoons black pepper
2 tablespoons Matouk's Hot Pepper Sauce

1. Mix all the ingredients in a large pot, making sure the brown sugar is well-blended.
2. Cook over low heat, stirring often, until heated through.

Note: This makes enough sauce for a mound of barbecue. Seasoned rice vinegar is available in the Oriental-foods section of most supermarkets. Matouk's Hot Pepper Sauce is available in Caribbean or West Indian markets.

Richard Ousey's Lip Smackin' Rib Sauce

Yield: 5 cups.

4 cups tomato sauce
1 tablespoon Louisiana Hot Sauce
1 tablespoon chili powder
1/2 cup light brown sugar
1 large lemon
2 large cloves garlic
1/2 cup soy sauce
1 ounce butter

1. Combine all ingredients, except garlic and lemon in a 3-quart stainless steel, glass or enamel saucepan.

Squeeze juice into sauce, being careful to discard seeds. Add the lemon hulls to the sauce. Peel the garlic by smacking them with the flat side of the blade of a chef's knife. Discard the papery husk and add the cracked garlic to the sauce.
3. Bring sauce to a boil over low heat. Simmer uncovered until slightly thickened. Before using, remove lemon hulls and garlic with a slotted spoon.

Note: Brush on grilled ribs, steak, pork chops or chicken. It's also good on baked meat or meat cooked in a smoker. Refrigerate unused portion.

Spencer's Blackberry Barbecue Sauce

Yield: 3/4 cup

1/2 cup Marsala wine
1/2 cup white wine
3 ounces blackberry jelly
3 tablespoons Worcestershire sauce, divided
1/4 teaspoon white pepper
2 tablespoons soy sauce

1. In a saucepan, combine Marsala, white wine, jelly, 2 tablespoons of the Worcestershire sauce and white pepper.
2. Simmer mixture until volume is reduced to half the original amount. Add soy sauce and remaining tablespoon of Worcestershire sauce. Mix well and use as a baste for chicken, fish or pork.

Karen Sullivan's Deep-South Gentlemen's Juice

Yield: 1 1/3 cups

1/4 tablespoon butter
2 green onions
3 tablespoons dark brown sugar
2 ounces Jack Daniels whiskey
1/4 orange juice
1 teaspoon lime juice
1 cup ketchup
1 1/2 teaspoons Lousiana-style red
 pepper sauce
Dash each salt and pepper

1. In a saucepan, melt butter over low heat.
2. Using the firm white/light green part of the onions only, finely chop the green onion. Saute chopped onions in butter over medium heat until onions begin to brown.
3. Turn burner to low heat. Add brown sugar to pan. Stir until sugar darkens and clumps. Be careful no to burn sugar.
4. Turn burner off. Add whiskey. Stir until sugar is completely dissolved.
5. Add the remaining ingredients in the order listed, mixing well after each addition. Heat over medium-low heat until mixture simmers. Decrease heat to low and continue cooking mixture for at least 15 minutes, stirring as needed.

Enrique Perez's Cubana Barbecue Sauce

Yield: 2 cups

1 medium white onion, chopped
5 cloves garlic, chopped
1/2 cup sour orange juice or 1/3 cup lime juice
1/2 teaspoon oregano
1/2 teaspoon cumin seeds
1/4 teaspoon salt
1/2 cup water

1. Put onions, garlic, orange juice (or lime juice) and water in a blender. Set blender on "liquify" setting and process.
2. Crush all dry ingredients together and add them to the blender. Process for 1 more minute.

Note: This is a traditional Cuban meat marinade. Sour orange juice is available in Hispanic grocery stores. Marinate meat (chicken, beef, pork or fish) for at least 1 hour in mixture. It is better to marinate meats overnight. Brush meat frequently with the sauce while cooking.

Dan E. Parma's Family Texas Bar-B-Q Sauce

Yield: about 1 quart

1 cup tomato ketchup
1/2 cup vinegar
1 teaspoon brown sugar
1 teaspoon chili powder
1/4 teaspoon salt
1 1/2 cups of water
3 celery stalks chopped
3 bay leaves
3/4 teaspoon cumin powder
1/2 lemon and peel
Dash of black pepper
1 teaspoon paprika
4 tablespoons Worcestershire sauce

4 tablespoons butter or margarine
1/2 onion, chopped
2 cloves garlic

1. Combine all ingredients in large sauce pan and bring to a boil. Simmer 10 to 15 minutes. Remove form heat and strain.

Dorothy Sayre's Barbecue Sauce

Yield: 4 1/2 quarts

1 cup salad oil
2 cups finely chopped celery
1 cup finely chopped parsley
2 cups finely chopped green bell pepper
2 teaspoons finely chopped mint
2 1/2 cups finely chopped onions
1 head garlic, peeled and finely chopped
4 cups ketchup
1 cup dark beer
1 pint pineapple juice
5 tablespoons prepared mustard
1 teaspoon salt or to taste
1 pint water
2 tablespoons liquid smoke
1/4 cup Louisiana hot sauce
12 ounces hot V-8 juice
2 cups dark brown sugar
1/2 cup red-wine vinegar
6 tablespoons Worcestershire sauce
1/2 cup honey
2 cups dark molasses

1. Heat 1 cup salad oil in a large Dutch oven. Saute celery, parsley, bell pepper, mint, onions and garlic.

2. Add ketchup, dark beer, pineapple juice, mustard, salt, water, liquid smoke, hot sauce, V-8 juice, brown sugar, red-wine vinegar, Worcestershire sauce honey and dark molasses.

3. Simmer, covered, for several hours, stirring occasionally until thickened. Mixture will burn on bottom of pan if not stirred.

A Dozen Great Grilling ideas

Orange-Cumin Marinade for Chicken

Orange-Cumin Marinade for Chicken

Yield: 4 servings

1/4 cup frozen orange juice concentrate
2 tablespoons water
2 teaspoons onion powder
1 teaspoon garlic powder
1 teaspoon ground cumin
3/4 teaspoon salt
1/8 teaspoon ground red pepper
1 1/4 pounds boned and skinned
chicken breasts (cutlets)

1. In a shallow glass baking dish, combine orange juice, water, onion and garlic powders, cumin, salt and red pepper.

2. Pierce chicken with fork tines on both sides. Add chicken to orange juice mixture, turning to coat on all sides. Set chicken aside, covered, for 10 to 15 minutes.

3. Pour excess marinade into a small saucepan. Bring mixture to a boil. Lightly spray chicken with non-stick cooking spray.

4. Place chicken on a rack over hot coals. Grill, basting frequently with heated marinade, until juices run clear, 4 to 5 minutes on each side.

Grilled Trout With Sesame-Soy Butter

Yield: 4 servings

4 (4-ounce) trout fillets
3 tablespoons bottled teriyaki sauce
Sesame-soy butter:
2 tablespoons butter or margarine,
softened
2 tablespoons sesame seeds, toasted
1 1/2 teaspoons finely chopped green
  onion
3/4 teaspoon light soy sauce

1. Heat grill. Marinate trout in teriyaki sauce for 15 minutes in the refrigerator.

2. Combine ingredients listed for sesame-soy butter and set aside until ready to use.

3. Place fillets flesh-side down on an oiled grill over hot coals. Cook about 2 minutes. Gently turn trout with a spatula; continue to cook 2 minutes longer. Serve with dollop of sesame-soy butter.

Grilled Catfish With Black Bean Relish

Grilled Catfish With Black Bean Relish

Yield: 4 servings

4 farm-raised catfish fillets
1/2 teaspoon garlic salt
Freshly ground black pepper

1. Prepare a grill or preheat the broiler.
2. Sprinkle catfish with garlic salt and pepper. Place fish on an oiled rack or a broiler pan rack. Grill or broil about 4 inches from the heat source for about 5 minutes on each side, or until fish flakes easily with a fork.
3. Place grilled fish on serving plates and serve with the black bean relish.

Black Bean Relish

2 tablespoons butter or margarine
1/2 cup chopped onion
1/4 cup chopped celery
1/4 cup chopped carrot
3 garlic cloves, minced
3 jalapeno peppers, seeded and chopped
1 (15-ounce) can black beans, undrained
1/2 cup diced ham
1/4 cup chopped fresh cilantro or parsley
1/2 teaspoon salt

1. To make the relish, melt butter or margarine in a saucepan over medium heat. Add onion, celery, carrot, garlic and jalapeno peppers. Cook until onion is tender. Stir in black beans with liquid, ham, cilantro or parsley and salt. Bring to a boil. Reduce heat and simmer, uncovered, for 10 minutes, or until mixture reaches desired consistency. Set aside.

41

Onion Curry Burgers

Curry, garlic, onion and chutney are used to flavor these burgers.
Yield: 4 servings

1 pound lean ground beef
1/4 cup Major Grey Chutney, chopped
1 tablespoon curry powder
1 teaspoon garlic powder
1/2 teaspoon salt
1/3 cup instant minced onion

1. In a medium-size bowl, combine beef, chutney, curry powder, garlic powder and salt. Mix until just combined. Shape into 4 patties, about 3/4-inch thick.

2. In a pie plate, place minced onion. Press each burger into onion, turning to coat on each side.

3. Light coals. When coals are ready for grilling grill burgers about 4 inches over heat source for 4 to 5 minutes per side. (To broil: put burgers on a rack in broiling pan about 6 inches from the heat source, 4 to 5 minutes per side.)

Honey-Glazed Barbecued Spareribs

Yield: 4 to 6 servings.

4 pounds lean pork spareribs
Water
Salt and pepper
1/2 cup honey
1/4 cup lemon juice
2 teaspoons grated lemon peel
2 teaspoons grated ginger
1 clove garlic, minced
1 teaspoon rosemary, crushed
1/2 teaspoon crushed red chilies
1/2 teaspoon ground sage

1. Completely cover spareribs with water in a large pot or deep skillet. Bring to boil, uncovered, over medium heat. Simmer 4 minutes. Drain liquid, reserving it for stock for later use, if desired. Season both sides of spareribs with salt and pepper. Place spareribs on rack in roasting pan. Cover loosely with aluminum foil.

2. Bake at 450 F for 15 minutes.

3. Combine remaining ingredients; mix well. Reduce oven temperature to 350 F. Brush spareribs with honey mixture. Bake 1 hour longer or until fully cooked, brushing with honey mixture every 15 minutes.

To grill: Boil spareribs as described above, over medium heat. Simmer 4 minutes and drain liquid. Season both sides of spareribs with salt and pepper. Place spareribs on barbecue grill over hot coals. Cook approximately 30 minutes per side. Brush meat side generously with honey mixture twice during last 15 minutes of cooking time.

Maple Pepper Chops With Sizzling Applesauce

Maple Pepper Chops With Sizzling Applesauce

Add sizzle to a menu with this recipe. Round out the meal with grilled squash or slaw
Yield: 4 servings

4 pork chops, 1-inch thick
1/3 cup thawed apple juice concentrate
1/3 cup apple cider vinegar
1/3 cup maple syrup
1 1/2 teaspoons crumbled dried sage,
or 1/4 cup fresh snipped sage
1/2 teaspoon salt
1 tablespoon coarsely ground black
pepper

1. In a large resealable bag, mix together apple juice concentrate, 1/3 cup apple cider vinegar, maple syrup, sage, salt and pepper. Add pork chops and seal bag. Refrigerate 4-24 hours.

2. Prepare a fire in a grill. Remove chops from marinade. Discard any remaining marinade. Grill chops over direct heat for 10 minutes, turning once. Serve with applesauce.

Sizzling Applesauce

Sizzling applesauce:
3 large Granny Smith apples,
cored and sliced
1/2 cup sugar
1/4 cup apple cider vinegar
3/4 teaspoon salt
1 whole clove
1 cinnamon stick
1 jalapeno pepper, seeded and cut
in half (see note)

To make sizzling applesauce, combine apples, 1/2 cup sugar, 1/4 cup apple cider vinegar, 3/4 teaspoon salt, clove, cinnamon stick, jalapeno in a saucepan. Bring to a boil, lower heat, cover and simmer for 20 minutes, until apples are soft. Remove from heat. Discard clove and cinnamon stick. Puree mixture in the work bowl of a food processor or blender. Cover and let cool at room temperature up to 3 hours. If making ahead, cover and refrigerate for up to one week.

Note: Wear rubber cloves when working with jalapeno peppers.

Grilled Walnut-Stuffed Turkey Rolls

Yield: 6 servings.

Yogurt sauce:
1 1/2 cups nonfat plain yogurt
2 tablespoons lemon juice
2 tablespoons chopped ripe olives
2 teaspoons dried chives

Stuffing:
1 tablespoon olive oil or vegetable oil
1/2 cup chopped onion
1 (10-ounce) box frozen spinach, thawed
1 cup fresh white bread crumbs
3/4 cup finely chopped walnuts
1 teaspoon dried thyme
1/3 cup water or chicken broth
Salt
Freshly ground black pepper
6 to 8 skinless, boneless turkey breast slices, 1/4 to 1/3 inch thick
Nonstick cooking spray
Sprigs of parsley for garnish

1. To make the yogurt sauce: Stir together the yogurt, lemon juice, olives and chives; set aside until serving (refrigerate if the wait is more than one hour).

2. To make the stuffing: Heat the oil in a skillet. Add the onion; cook until soft, about 5 minutes. Put spinach in a strainer; press firmly to remove the excess liquid. Add the spinach to the skillet; cook 3 minutes more. Transfer the mixture to a large bowl. Add the bread crumbs, walnuts and thyme; then stir and toss with a fork to combine. Add the water or broth; stir until blended. Season with salt and pepper, if desired.

3. Place the turkey slices in a single layer on your work surface. Sprinkle with salt and pepper, if desired. Divide the filling evenly among the turkey, patting and spreading it over the top half of each slice. Starting from the filled end, roll up each slice pinwheel-style to enclose the stuffing and make a cylindrical, log-shaped roll. Coat the rolls lightly with nonstick cooking spray.

4. Prepare a barbecue fire. Grill the turkey rolls 4 to 6 inches from hot coals for about 15 minutes. Turn the rolls three or four times, until they are well-browned and the turkey is fully cooked (cut one in half if necessary to check its doneness).

5. Arrange the rolls on a platter. Spoon a small amount of sauce over the rolls, garnish with parsley and serve. Pass the remaining sauce at the table.

Tangy Marinated Vegetable Kabobs

Yield: 6 servings.

2 1/2 cups diagonally sliced zucchini
1 1/2 cups diagonally sliced yellow
 squash
1 red pepper, cut into 1-inch pieces
1 8-oz can artichoke hearts, drained
1/2 cup olive oil
1/4 cup freshly squeezed lemon juice
1 large clove garlic, minced
1/4 tsp salt
1/8 tsp freshly ground pepper

1. Place vegetables in large shallow baking dish. Combine oil, lemon juice, garlic, salt and pepper, mix well. Pour over vegetables and marinate 1 hour, tossing frequently.

2. Skewer vegetables on long wooden-handled skewers. Place on cooking grid of covered cooker over medium-hot charcoal briquettes, grill 5 to 7 minutes, turning and basting with marinade.

Lime-Scented Salmon

Yield: 4 servings.

1/3 cup olive or vegetable oil
1/4 cup lime juice
1/4 cup water
2 tablespoons instant minced onion
5 teaspoons ground cumin
1 teaspoon instant minced garlic
1 teaspoon salt
1/4 teaspoon ground black pepper
2 pounds salmon steaks, cut 1-inch thick
Lime wedges

1. In a shallow nonmetallic baking pan, combine oil, lime juice, water, onion, cumin, garlic, salt and black pepper.

2. Using a fork pierce salmon liberally on both sides. Put fish in marinade and turn to coat.

3. Cover pan and refrigerate for 20 minutes, or up to 2 hours.

4. Heat barbecue or broiler until hot. Remove fish from marinade. Heat marinade to boiling. Grill or broil fish 3 to 4 inches from heat until cooked, about 4 or 5 minutes per side.

5. Brush fish occasionally with cooked marinade. Serve with lime wedges and season with additional salt and black pepper.

Chicken and Potato Fiesta Grill

Yield: 4 servings.

1 1/3 pounds (4 medium) potatoes,
cut into 1 1/4 -inch cubes
1/2 cup fresh lime juice
1 tablespoon vegetable oil
2 cloves garlic, chopped
1 teaspoon chili powder
1 teaspoon dried oregano leaves
1 teaspoon salt
1/2 teaspoon ground cumin
1/2 teaspoon ground red pepper flakes
4 whole chicken legs with thighs
1 small red pepper, seeded and cut into
1 1/2 -inch squares
2 medium (6-inch) zucchini, cut into
3/4 -inch slices
1/4 pound button mushrooms
4 to 8 warm flour or corn tortillas
Prepared salsa

1. Combine potato cubes and 2 tablespoons water in a microwave-safe dish. Cover, cook on high (100 percent power) about 10 minutes, until potatoes are just tender; cool.

2. For the marinade: In a small bowl, whisk lime juice, oil, garlic, chili powder, oregano, salt, cumin and pepper flakes. Pour 1/4 cup marinade over chicken in resealable plastic bag; turn to coat chicken. Set aside 30 minutes, or refrigerate up to two hours.

3. Thread potato cubes, bell pepper squares, zucchini slices and mushrooms alternately onto eight 10-to-12-inch bamboo skewers. Place on baking pan; brush with remaining marinade to coat.

4. Remove chicken from plastic bag; reserve marinade. Grill chicken over glowing coals 30 to 40 minutes, basting with its marinade. Be sure to discard any uncooked marinade. Turn chicken as needed, until juices run clear.

5. About 10 minutes before chicken is done, place skewers on grill. Cook, turning and basting occasionally with vegetable marinade until hot through and lightly browned. Potato skewers and chicken can be cooked under a broiler rather than on a grill, if you choose. Potatoes and vegetables can be wrapped in tortillas or eaten as desired. Serve salsa on the side.

Ducky's Wild Duck With Port Sauce

This recipe was created by Dan Duckhorn of Duckhorn Vineyards in St. Helena, California

1/2 duck per person
Orange juice
Lemon juice
1 bottle California port (Ficklin's preferred)
1 cup orange juice
Juice of 1 lemon
2 cloves garlic, crushed
1 1/2 teaspoons Worcestershire sauce
4 teaspoons concentrated liquid beef bouillon (Bovril)
1 thinly sliced red onion
2 slices red or green bell pepper
2 heaping teaspoons Major Grey's peach chutney
4 heaping teaspoons blackberry seedless jam
1/2 cup frozen butter
Salt and pepper to taste
Mixed herbs of choice

1. Salt and pepper ducks. Rub with mixed herbs. Squeeze orange and lemon juice over ducks. Grill, bone side down, over very hot coals for 8-10 minutes. Turn and grill for 6-8 minutes breast side down. Keep water on hand to keep flames under control. Breasts should be firm to the touch, when done. Place on a warmed platter. Set aside.

2. Bring port wine to a simmer. Add 1 cup orange and juice of 1 lemon. Let mixture simmer for 15 minutes over medium heat.

3. Add garlic, Worcestershire sauce and liquid beef bouillon. Float one thin slice of red onion and two strips of the red bell pepper in the sauce. Add peach chutney, blackberry jam and a dash of mixed herbs of choice. Season to taste with salt and pepper.

4. Cook sauce over low heat until volume is reduced by half. Strain sauce and continue cooking over low heat until it reaches a dark brown, syrup consistency. Add frozen butter in small pieces, stirring until each piece is well-combined. Spoon over warm, grilled duck with wild rice and sauteed greens.

49

Grilled Sirloin With Pimento Butter

Yield: 4 servings

4-ounce jar pimentos, rinsed and patted dry
1 shallot, finely chopped
1 1/2 tablespoons chopped fresh tarragon (or 2 teaspoons dried tarragon)
1/2 pound sweet butter, at room temperature
Salt and pepper to taste
2 sirloin steaks, 2 pounds each, sliced 2 inches thick

1. Finely chop pimentos and combine with shallot, tarragon and butter; blend well. Season to taste with salt and pepper. Place mixture on plastic wrap and form into log shape. Wrap tightly and refrigerate until ready to use.

2. Prepare grill. Oil cooking grid when coals are ready. Sear steaks 30 seconds on each side. Cook steaks to desired doneness (7-9 minutes per side for rare, 9-12 minutes per side for medium, 12-15 minutes per side for well-done), turning only once after searing. Serve steak with pimento butter on top.

Note: Freeze remaining butter for another use.

Side Dishes and Salads

SALAD DRESSING

Antipasto Garden Salad

Antipasto Garden Salad

Yield: 8 servings

1 pound penne pasta, uncooked
1 (12-ounce) jar roasted red peppers,
 rinsed, drained, cut into thin strips
1 (12-ounce) jar marinated artichoke
 hearts drained, coarsely chopped
1 cup diced Muenster or Provolone
 cheese
1 cup sliced mushrooms
1/2 cup chopped red onion
1/3 cup chopped fresh basil
2/3 cup low-fat Caesar or Italian salad
 dressing
Freshly ground black pepper
Sliced pepperoncini peppers (optional)

1. Prepare pasta according to package directions.
2. While pasta is cooking, combine pepper strips, artichoke hearts, cheese, mushrooms, onion and basil in a large bowl.
3. Drain pasta and rinse under cold water.
4. Combine pasta and dressing to the large bowl. Toss well. Cover and refrigerate for at least 1 hour before serving. Sprinkle with freshly ground black pepper and sliced pepperoncini peppers.

Pondo's Basil Tomatoes

Pondo's is a longtime favorite restaurant Volusia County, Florida.
Basil Tomatoes can also be served tossed with lightly cooked green beans.
Yield: 4 servings

4 vine ripe, never refrigerated tomatoes
 cut into wedges
Marinade:
2 tablespoons red-wine vinegar
1/2 cup olive oil
Salt and pepper to taste
1 teaspoon diced fresh garlic
2 tablespoons chopped fresh basil or
 1 teaspoon dried basil

1. Whisk together marinade ingredients.
2. Add tomato wedges and marinate 2 hours, covered, at room temperature. Marinade can be reserved, and more tomatoes added for another batch.

Apple Crunch Coleslaw

Yield: 6 to 8 servings

2 Golden Delicious or Granny Smith apples, cored and coarsely grated
8 ounces (about 2 3/4 cups) red or green cabbage, or combination of the two, cored and cut into thin slivers
1 carrot, pared and shredded
1 green or red pepper, shredded
1/3 cup mayonnaise
2 to 3 teaspoons vinegar
2 teaspoons milk
1 1/2 teaspoons Dijon mustard
Dash sugar
Salt and pepper

1. Combine apples, cabbage, carrot and pepper.
2. In another bowl, combine mayonnaise, vinegar, milk, mustard, sugar, and salt and pepper to taste; mix well.
3. Toss with apple mixture.

Recipe note: Salad can be refrigerated, covered, up to 24 hours.

Black-Eyed Susan Salad

Yield: 6 servings

1 (15-ounce) can black-eyed peas, drained
1 (10-ounce) package frozen whole kernel corn, thawed
1 small green pepper, diced
1 small sweet red pepper, diced, or 2 tbsps diced pimento
1/2 cup diced celery
2 tablespoons very finely chopped onion
1/4 cup cider vinegar
1/4 cup oil
1 tablespoon sugar

2 tablespoons Worcestershire sauce
1/2 teaspoon garlic salt
1/8 teaspoon pepper

1. Combine peas, corn, green and red pepper, celery and onion in medium-size bowl.
2. Combine remaining ingredients for dressing.
3. Pour dressing over vegetables; toss. Chill several hours in refrigerator. If desired, serve on lettuce leaves garnished with sweet bell pepper rings.

Grilled Tomato and Mozzarella Salad

Yield: 4 servings

2 large beefsteak tomatoes, thickly sliced
Salt and freshly ground pepper
3 tablespoons extra-virgin olive oil
1/4 pound mozzarella cheese, thinly sliced
1/4 cup finely chopped fresh basil or parsley

1. Prepare a medium-hot fire. Season tomatoes with salt and pepper.

2. Brush 1 side of each slice with olive oil. Set tomatoes oiled side down on an oiled grill and cook without turning for about 2 minutes, until very lightly browned. Brush lightly with olive oil and turn carefully with a wide metal spatula.

3. Place a piece of mozzarella on top of each tomato slice and grill, covered, until cheese just begins to melt and tomatoes are softened but still hold their shape, about 2 minutes longer.

4. Transfer cheese-topped tomato slices to a platter. Sprinkle basil over tomatoes and drizzle on remining olive oil.

New Potato Salad With Peas

Yield: 6 servings

1 1/2 pounds red new potatoes, cooked and drained
Salt
1 cup fresh peas (or thawed frozen peas), partially cooked
1/2 cup sliced celery
2 tablespoons finely minced onion
Vinaigrette dressing:
1/2 cup vegetable oil
1/3 cup tarragon wine vinegar
1 tablespoon chopped parsley
1 teaspoon Dijon mustard
Salt and pepper to taste

1. To make vinaigrette dressing, combine vegetable oil, tarragon wine vinegar, chopped parsley, Dijon mustard, salt and pepper; mix well. Makes 2/3 cup.

2. Do not peel potatoes; salt lightly and marinate while still warm in 1/3 cup of the vinaigrette dressing. Refrigerate until thoroughly chilled. Toss together with remaining ingredients; add additional vinaigrette dressing if necessary.

Summer Pasta Salad

Yield: 4 servings

1 head romaine lettuce
4 ounces tortellini or pasta shells
1 to 2 quarts boiling salted water
2 large carrots, peeled and cut into thin
  matchsticks
1/2 cup vegetable oil
1/4 cup soy sauce
1/4 cup lemon juice
1 medium garlic clove
1 teaspoon grated fresh ginger
1 cup cherry tomatoes, halved
1/2 cup minced green onion
2 tablespoons toasted sesame seeds
  (optional)

1. Core, rinse and thoroughly drain lettuce; chill in plastic bag or plastic crisper.

2. Add tortellini to boiling water. Return to boil, reduce heat and simmer until tender, about 20 minutes. Drain, then run under cold water until cool. Drain again.

3. Steam carrots in small amount of water until slightly tender, about 3 or 4 minutes. Drain and run under cold water to cool. Combine pasta and carrots in bowl.

4. Combine oil, soy sauce, lemon juice, garlic and ginger in blender and blend until mixture is smooth. Pour 1/2 cup of mixture over pasta and carrots. Add tomatoes and onion. Cover and chill. Tear enough lettuce to make 1 quart. Arrange lettuce on a platter. Top with pasta mixture. Sprinkle with sesame seeds, if desired. Pass remaining dressing separately.

Five-Cup Wonder Salad

Yield: 6 servings

1 cup green seedless grapes
1 cup red seedless grapes
2 cups torn lettuce leaves
1 cup shredded carrots
Honey lime dressing:
1/3 cup lime juice
1/4 cup honey
1 teaspoon grated lime peel
1 teaspoon salt
Dash of cayenne pepper

1. In a large bowl, mix grapes, lettuce and carrots.

2. Combine dressing ingredients. Toss with grape mixture. Makes about 1/2 cup.

Grilled Herbed Corn

Yield: 4 servings

8 ears corn
1/4 pound butter, at room temperature
1/4 cup chopped fresh herbs (such as
  parsley, chives, thyme or oregano)
Salt and pepper to taste

1. Carefully peel back husks of corn, leaving them attached at base. Remove silk. Combine butter, herbs, salt and pepper; blend well.

2. Spread mixture generously over corn. Pull husk back up over corn. Cook over prepared barbecue 12-15 minutes, turning occasionally.

58

Cilantro Butter for Corn

Yield: 4 servings

1 tablespoon cilantro, chopped
1 cup butter, softened
Pinch white pepper
Pinch ground cumin

1. Combine all ingredients in a food processor or blender. Blend until mixed.
2. Refrigerate overnight.

Note: Fresh basil, mint, oregano, rosemary or thyme may be used instead of cilantro.

Cajun Butter

Yield: 6 servings

2 tablespoons paprika
1 teaspoon cayenne pepper
1/2 teaspoon thyme, ground
1/2 teaspoon onion powder
1/2 teaspoon garlic powder
1/2 teaspoon sage, ground
1/2 teaspoon white pepper
1 teaspoon sugar
1 cup butter, softened

1. Combine all ingredients in a food processor or blender. Blend until thoroughly mixed.
2. Refrigerate overnight before serving.

Note: This is a fairly spicy mix. If you don't like hot food, reduce the amount of cayenne pepper by half.

Garlic Butter

Yield: 4 servings

1/4 cup shallots, chopped
1 to 2 cloves garlic
1 tablespoon parsley
1/8 to 1/4 teaspoon salt
Pepper to taste
1 cup butter

1. In a food processor or blender, combine shallots, garlic, parsley, salt and pepper. Blend to a fine paste.
2. Beat in butter until thoroughly mixed. Refrigerate overnight.

Note: This doubles as a wonderful melted dip for escargot.

Tomato, Curry and Orange Butter

Yeild: 10 servings

2 cups butter, softened
2 tablespoons tomato puree
1/2 teaspoon grated fresh orange rind
Salt to taste
1 heaping teaspoon mild, good-quality
Madras curry powder

1. Combine all ingredients in a food processor or blender. Blend until thoroughly mixed.
2. Refrigerate overnight before using.

Sesame Butter

Yield: 4 to 6 servings

1 cup butter, softened
3 tablespoon sesame seeds, toasted and cooled to room temperature
1 teaspoon sesame oil
1 teaspoon rice vinegar
Pinch salt

1. Combine ingredients in a blender or food processor. Beat until smooth.
2. Refrigerate before serving.

Tuscan Bean Stew

Yield: 4 (1 1/4 -cup) servings

3 tablespoons extra-virgin olive oil
2 teaspoons ground sage
3 garlic cloves, minced
1 (15-ounce) can black beans, drained, rinsed
1 (15-ounce) can red kidney beans, drained, rinsed
1 (28-ounce) can Italian-style peeled plum tomatoes with basil, undrained, cut up
1/3 cup dry red wine
1/2 teaspoon salt
1/4 teaspoon pepper

1. Heat oil in Dutch oven or three-quart saucepan over medium heat until hot. Add sage and garlic, cook and stir 2-3 minutes or until garlic is tender.
2. Stir in remaining ingredients, simmer 15-20 minutes or until slightly thickened, stirring occasionally.

Casablanca Couscous

Yield: 4 servings

1 (14-ounce) can vegetable or chicken broth
1/2 cup diced dried apricots
1/4 teaspoon ground pepper
1 1/2 cups couscous
1 cup halved seedless grapes
1/3 cup toasted coarsely chopped pistachios
2 tablespoons minced parsley

1. Bring broth, apricots and pepper to boil in medium saucepan.
2. Stir in couscous and grapes and cover saucepan. Remove from heat and let stand 5 minutes.
3. Add pistachios and parsley; lightly fluff mixture with fork.

Chef Patrick Reilly's Smart Caesar Salad

Yield: 6 servings

1 (8-ounce) container of low-fat or fat-free yogurt
1 tablespoon freshly chopped garlic
1 tablespoon Dijon mustard
2 tablespoons red-wine vinegar
1 tablespoon lemon juice
1 teaspoon sugar
3 tablespoons freshly grated Parmesan cheese
Salt to taste
White pepper to taste
Freshly ground black pepper to taste
1 tablespoon extra-virgin olive oil (optional)
1 head romaine lettuce

1. Put yogurt in a sieve over a bowl and allow excess liquid to drain off. Transfer remaining yogurt to a mixing bowl. Add chopped garlic, mustard, red-wine vinegar, lemon juice, sugar, Parmesan cheese, salt, white pepper, black pepper and olive oil. Mix well.

2. Tear clean romaine lettuce leaves into bite-size pieces. Blot dry on a clean dish towel.

3. Combine yogurt mixture and lettuce leaves, tossing to coat. Divide mixture between 6 salad plates.

Croutons

1 loaf French bread cut into 12 (1/2-inch) slices
2 cloves garlic
Olive oil cooking spray

1. Rub both sides of bread slices with garlic cloves. Spray very lightly with olive oil-flavored spray. Bake in a 375 F oven until crisp or grill over hot coals, turning to evenly brown.

2. Garnish each plate with 2 croutons.

Donna McGregor Fant's Potato Salad

Yield: 6 servings

6 medium-size red potatoes
1 teaspoon salt
1/2 teaspoon pepper
1/4 teaspoon celery seed
1/2 teaspoon dill
2 tablespoons sugar
1 1/2 tablespoons light-colored vinegar
1/4 teaspoon onion powder
1/2 cup fat-free yogurt
1/2 cup mayonnaise
1/2 cup chopped red bell pepper
1/2 cup chopped green onions (green and white parts)
3 hard boiled eggs, peeled and sliced
Paprika

1. Cook potatoes in boiling water until fork-tender. Spread potatoes out on a baking sheet to cool. Quarter or cut cooled potatoes in half. Place in a large mixing bowl.

2. Combine salt, pepper, celery seed, dill, sugar, vinegar and onion powder. Sprinkle over potatoes.

3. Combine yogurt, mayonnaise, red bell pepper and green onions. Fold mixture into potatoes. Arrange sliced eggs over top and sprinkle with paprika. Serve chilled.

Grilled Blue Cheese Potatoes

Yield: 6 servings

6 baking potatoes
6 slices bacon
1 cup sliced onion
3/4 cup crumbled blue cheese

1. Pierce potatoes with fork. Place potatoes on cooking grid of covered cooker over medium-hot charcoal briquettes. Close grill cover and cook 60 minutes or until done. Move potatoes to outside edge of cooking grid or to warming rack.

2. Cook bacon in a skillet over charcoal briquettes until crisp. Remove bacon from skillet and crumble. Add onion slices to bacon fat in skillet. Cook until golden brown.

3. Split potatoes open. Spoon onions onto steaming potatoes. Sprinkle with crumbled bacon and top with cheese. Close grill cover and cook potatoes just until cheese melts.

Radish and Orange Salad

Radish and Orange Salad

Yield: 4 servings

1 (6-ounce) bag radishes, sliced (about 2 cups)
2 (11-ounce) cans Mandarin oranges, drained (about 1 1/2 cups)
1 cup sliced celery
1/2 cup thinly sliced red onion
2 tablespoons chopped parsley
1/4 cup bottled honey-Dijon dressing

1. Combine radishes, oranges, celery, onion and parsley in a medium-size bowl. Toss with dressing.

Warm Chicken and Radish Salad With Wilted Romaine

Yield: 4 servings

1 tablespoon vegetable oil
1 pound boned and skinned chicken breasts, cut into thin strips
1/2 teaspoon salt
2 cups mixed sliced sweet red and yellow bell peppers
1 teaspoon minced garlic
1 1/2 cups (about 6 ounces) radishes, quartered
1/4 cup green onions, cut diagonally into 1-inch pieces
2 cups torn Romaine lettuce
1/2 cup bottled red-wine vinaigrette

1. In a large skillet over medium-high heat, heat oil until hot. Add chicken and sprinkle with salt. Cook and stir until browned on all sides, about 5 minutes. Transfer chicken to a plate, covering to keep warm.

2. In the same skillet, cook and stir peppers and garlic until tender, about 8 minutes. Stir in radishes and green onions. Cook until barely crisp-tender, about 3 minutes longer. Stir in lettuce and chicken. Heat until lettuce wilts slightly, about 1 minute.

3. Remove from heat and toss with red-wine vinaigrette. Serve immediately.

Cheese-Stuffed Chilies With Tomato Corn Salsa

Yield: 8 servings

1 cup low-fat cottage cheese
1/2 cup shredded Cheddar cheese
1/2 cup chopped green onion
1 1/2 teaspoons chili powder, or more, as desired
8 large pasilla or anaheim chilies
Salt

1. Combine cheeses, onion and chili powder; set aside. Grill chilies over medium coals, turning until charred. Place in plastic bag to steam. Peel off blackened skin. Cut slit in side; remove seeds, leaving stems on both for appearance and to hold the chilies together while they cook.

2. Stuff chilies with cheese mixture; return to grill. Turn carefully until cheese is melted and hot. Serve with Tomato Corn Salsa.

Note: To prepare in a conventional oven, use broiler to char the chilies before peeling skin. Bake stuffed chilies in a 400 F oven for about 5 minutes until cheese is melted and hot.

Tomato Corn Salsa

4 plum tomatoes, chopped
1 clove garlic, minced
1 small jalapeno chili, seeded and minced
1/2 cup fresh corn kernels
2 tablespoons chopped cilantro
1 tablespoon lime juice or lemon juice
Salt

1. Combine ingredients. Add salt as desired.

Note: Add more chili powder to make spicier. For more smoky flavor, grill jalapeno, corn and tomatoes.

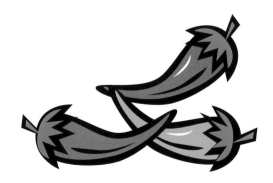

Fiesta Bean Salad

Yield: 6-8 servings

2 cups cold cooked rice
1 (16-ounce) can kidney beans, rinsed
 and drained
1 cup fresh cooked or frozen corn
kernels, thawed, or 1 (8-ounce) can of
corn, drained
1/2 cup sliced green onions with tops
1 medium red bell pepper, cut into 1-by-
1/4 inch strips (1 1/2 cups)
1/2 to 2/3 cup bottled picante sauce
1/4 cup Italian dressing
1 teaspoon ground cumin
1/2 teaspoon salt

1. Combine rice, beans, corn, red pepper and green onions in a bowl.
2. Combine picante sauce, dressing, cumin and salt. Pour over rice mixture; toss. Cover and chill.

Onion Bread and Butter Pickles

Yield: 8 pints

6 medium (3 pounds) sweet Spanish
 onions
3 quarts (about 5 pounds) pickling
 cucumbers, sliced 1/4-inch thick
1/3 cup salt
3 cups vinegar
3 cups sugar
1 1/2 teaspoons turmeric
2 tablespoons mustard seed
1 1/2 teaspoons celery seed

1. Peel and slice onions 1/4-inch thick. Separate into rings.
2. Arrange onions and cucumbers in layers in a large bowl, sprinkling each layer with salt. Cover top with ice cubes and mix thoroughly. Let stand 3 to 4 hours. Drain well.
3. Combine vinegar, sugar, and spices in large kettle. Bring to boil. Add onins and cucumbers. Return to boil.
4. Pack into hot sterilized jars, leaving 1/4-inch head space. Adjust caps. Process in boiling water bath for 10 minutes.

Dilled Cucumber Salad

Yield: 2 to 3 servings

1 large cucumber, thinly sliced
1/2 red onion, thinly sliced
1/3 cup white vinegar
2 tablespoons vegetable oil
1/2 teaspoon seasoned salt
1 teaspoon sugar
1 teaspoon ground black pepper
4 tablespoons chopped fresh dill

1. Place cucumber and red onion in a shallow bowl.

2. In a small bowl, stir together white vinegar, vegetable oil, seasoned salt, sugar and ground black pepper. Mix until all sugar dissolves. Pour over cucumbers and onions.

3. Add dill and toss gently. Let sit at room temperature for an hour.

Black-Eyed Pea, Green Pea and Rice Salad

Yield: 6 servings.

1 cup diced carrots
1 cup frozen green peas, thawed
1/4 cup olive oil
3 tablespoons lemon juice
2 tablespoons water
1 teaspoon mustard
1/2 teaspoon salt
1/4 teaspoon red pepper sauce
3 cups cooked long-grain white rice
1 (16-ounce) can black-eyed peas, drained, rinsed
1/2 cup diced celery
1/2 cup diced sweet yellow onion
1/2 cup diced red bell pepper
1/4 finely chopped parsley
Freshly ground black pepper to taste

1. Heat a saucepan half filled with water to a boil. Stir in carrots and boil, uncovered, for 2 minutes. Add peas to the carrots and boil, uncovered, 1 minute. Drain and rinse with cold water. Set aside.

2. Whisk oil, lemon juice, 2 tablespoons water, mustard, salt and pepper sauce in a large bowl until blended.

3. Add the black-eyed peas, rice, carrots, peas, celery, onion, bell pepper and parsley to the dressing. Add black pepper to taste. Toss to blend. Let stand 20 minutes before serving.

Pasta With Pesto, Green Beans and Potatoes

Yield: 6 servings.

1 pound linguine or other pasta
2 cups diced new potatoes
2 cups halved trimmed green beans
1 large clove garlic
2 cups lightly packed fresh basil leaves
1/4 cup water
1/4 cup pine nuts
1/4 cup grated imported Parmesan
2 tablespoons olive oil
1/2 teaspoon salt
1/2 teaspoon freshly ground black pepper

1. Cook pasta according to package directions. Drain; keep warm.

2. Cook potatoes and green beans in a large saucepan of boiling water, uncovered, until crisp-tender, about 8 minutes. Drain; keep warm.

3. While noodles and vegetables cook, drop garlic into food processor or blender with machine running to finely chop it. Then add basil, 1/4 cup water, nuts, Parmesan, oil, salt and pepper. Process until basil is very finely chopped, almost pureed.

4. Toss pasta with potatoes, green beans and basil sauce to coat.

Red and Yellow Potato Salad with Bacon

Yield: 2 servings

1 large red potato, peeled and cut into 1/2-inch cubes
1 large sweet potato, peeled and cut into 1/2-inch cubes
Salt and pepper to taste
2 tablespoons white-wine vinegar
4 teaspoons Dijon-style honey mustard
1/2 teaspoon hot pepper sauce
4 tablespoons olive oil
3 slices fried bacon, drained well and crumbled
1/4 cup finely chopped celery

1. Boil potatoes (or cook in a microwave oven) until just tender, about 7 to 8 minutes. Drain, season with salt and pepper, and place in a medium-size bowl.

2. Whisk together white-wine vinegar, Dijon-style honey mustard, hot pepper sauce and olive oil.

3. Pour mustard mixture over cooked potatoes. Add crumbled bacon and celery. Toss well to distribute ingredients evenly.

Baked Sweet Onions

Yield: 1 servings

1 jumbo sweet Vidalia onion
1 tablespoon butter
1 beef bouillon cube
Dash salt
Dash pepper

1. Heat oven to 350 F. Core onion. Fill hollow with butter, bouillon, salt and pepper.
2. Wrap onion in foil and bake for 45 minutes. Do not overbake or onion will become tough. Serve with grilled steak.

Sweet Onion Gravy

Yield: 8 to 10 servings

3 cups chopped sweet Vidalia onions
1/2 cup bacon drippings
Salt to taste
1 teaspoon pepper
1 cup water
4 tablespoons all-purpose flour

1. Combine onions and bacon drippings in a skillet. Add salt and pepper and saute until onions are tender.
2. Mix flour with enough water to make a slightly thick paste. Slowly add to onion mixture. Continue cooking, stirring often, until mixture reaches the desired gravy consistency.

Ambrosia Stuffed Sweet Potatoes

Yield: 2 servings

1 medium sweet potato (about 8 ounces)
3 tablespoons light sour cream
2 tablespoons marshmallow creme
1 tablespoon sweetened flaked coconut
1 tablespoon chopped pecans
4 teaspoons drained, crushed pineapple
4 dried apricot halves, chopped

1. Heat oven to 400 F.

2. Wash the sweet potato, pat dry and pierce in several places with a fork. Bake for 45 to 50 minutes in a 400 F oven or cook in a microwave oven on high (100 percent power) for 5 minutes to 7 minutes, or until tender when pricked with a fork. Let cool slightly.

3. Combine the remaining ingredients in a bowl; blend well. Working lengthwise, slice sweet potato in half. Use a spoon to scoop out all but 1/4 inch of the flesh from each half. Place the scooped-out potato in a bowl, mash lightly with a fork; add about one-half of the ambrosia mixture to the mashed sweet potato; blend well. Spoon this mixture back into the potato skins and top each with the remaining ambrosia.

Sweet potato tips

● Available year-round, sweet potatoes can be baked, broiled, sauteed, fried or boiled. They can be substituted for Irish potatoes, apples or squash in almost any recipe. They can also be served raw, shredded on greens and cut into thin slices and served in salads.

● Select well-shaped, firm sweet potatoes.

● Never refrigerate uncooked sweet potatoes. Cool temperatures can cause damage. Store sweet potatoes in a dry, well-ventilated place. Use them within a week or two of purchase. Always cut them with a stainless steel knife. Carbon blades can cause the sweet potatoes to darken.

Thyme-Scented Green Olives, Piquillo Wrapped Shrimp, Spanish Cheese Tartlets and Potato Salad Espanol

Thyme-scented Green Olives

Yield: 3 cups

1 (10-ounce) jar pitted Spanish green olives, drained
1/4 cup olive oil
1 tablespoon chopped fresh thyme or
 1 teaspoon dried thyme
2 cloves garlic, minced

1. In a medium bowl, combine olives, olive oil, thyme and garlic. Cover and refrigerate at least 24 hours before serving. Serve at room temperature.

Piquillo Wrapped Shrimp with Saffron Aioli

Yield: 16-20 wrapped shrimp and 1/2 cup aioli

1/2 cup mayonnaise
2 tablespoons chopped parsley
1 tablespoon chopped drained capers
1 tablespoon lemon juice
1 small clove garlic, mashed to a puree
1/8 teaspoon saffron, crushed
1 pound large shrimp (about 16-20), shelled and deveined
2 teaspoons paprika
3/4 teaspoon salt
1/3 cup piquillo peppers or roasted red peppers cut in 1/2-inch strips
2 tablespoons olive oil

1. In a small bowl combine mayonnaise, parsley, capers, lemon juice, garlic and saffron; cover and refrigerate until ready to use.

2. Sprinkle shrimp with paprika and salt. Wrap each shrimp with a strip of piquillo pepper; fasten with a toothpick.

3. In a large skillet over medium-high heat, heat olive oil. Add half of the shrimp; cook, just until center is opaque, about 3 minutes, turning once; remove from skillet. Repeat with remaining shrimp adding oil if needed. Serve with Saffron Aioli.

Note: To broil, place pepper-wrapped shrimp, without toothpicks on a rack in a broiler pan; brush with olive oil; broil just until center is opaque, about 3 minutes.

Spanish Cheese & Spinach Tartlets

Yield: 2 dozen tartlets

6 slices thin white bread
1 (10-ounce) package frozen chopped
  spinach, thawed and squeezed dry
1 cup heavy (whipping) cream
3/4 cup cabrales cheese or shredded
  manchego cheese (about 3 ounces)
1/2 teaspoon salt
1/4 teaspoon ground black pepper
1/8 teaspoon ground nutmeg
2 tablespoons pine nuts, toasted
*To toast pine nuts: Place in a small dry
skillet over medium heat until golden, stirring often.*

1. Heat oven to 400 F. Lightly oil 24 (1
3/4-inch wide) minimuffin cups (holds 2
tablespoons liquid).

2. With a 1-1/2 inch cookie cutter, cut out 24
rounds from bread. Place rounds on a cookie
sheet; bake until just pale gold, turning once, about
5 minutes. Gently press toasted rounds into the bottom of muffin cups; set aside.

3. In a medium bowl combine spinach, cream,
cheese, salt, pepper and nutmeg until blended.
Spoon cheese mixture into bread cups; sprinkle
each with pine nuts. Bake until filling is set, about
15 minutes. Remove to a wire rack to cool slightly.
Serve warm.

*Note: The baked tartlets may be frozen in a tight-
ly covered container; to reheat, place frozen
tartlets on a pan in a 400 F oven until hot, about
10 minutes.*

Potato Salad Español

Yield: About 6 cups

2 pounds small red potatoes, halved or
  quartered
1/2 cup sliced pimento stuffed Spanish
  green olives
1/2 cup chopped fresh basil or 2 tablespoons dried basil
1/4 cup finely chopped red onion
2 tablespoons drained capers
2 teaspoons dried oregano, crushed
1 teaspoon salt

1/2 teaspoon ground black pepper
1/4 cup extra-virgin olive oil

1. Place potatoes in water to cover and bring to
a boil. Reduce heat and simmer, covered, until
potatoes are tender, about 15 minutes. Drain potatoes and transfer to a large bowl.

2. Add olives, basil, onion, capers, oregano,
salt and pepper and olive oil. Let stand for 30 minutes to allow flavors to meld.

Bistro Cappuccino's Vine-Ripe Tomato and Fresh Mozzarella Salad

Bistro Cappuccino is a popular eatery in Lake Mary, Florida.
Yields: 6 servings

3 vine-ripe beefsteak tomatoes
1 Bermuda onion
3 pieces fresh mozzarella
Marinade of olive oil, chopped basil and black pepper (enough to cover mozzarella)

Cut tomatoes into 6 (1/2-inch) slices. Slice onion into 6 (1/4-inch) thick slices. Cut each mozzarella piece into 4 slices and marinate in olive oil, basil and black pepper mixture.

Dressing

2 egg yolks
1 tablespoon Dijon mustard
Juice of 2 lemons
2 shallots, chopped
2 tablespoons chopped garlic
1/4 pound chopped basil
1 teaspoon black pepper
1 teaspoon salt
2 cups extra-virgin olive oil
Fresh basil for garnish

1. Combine yolk, mustard, lemon juice, pepper, salt, shallots and garlic. While whisking mixture, slowly add in 2 cups oil. Stir in basil. Let mixture stand in refrigerator for 1 hour.
2. Arrange salad on a cold plate by alternating slices of cheese, tomato and onions. Drizzle with dressing. Garnish with fresh basil.

Baked Bean Stew

Baked Bean Stew

Yeild: 8 servings

1 cup chopped onion
1 cup chopped green pepper
1 tablespoon vegetable oil
12 ounces boneless skinless chicken
 breast or tenders, cut into 1/2 inch
 pieces
2 cans (15 ounces each) baked
 beans or pork and beans
1 can (15 ounces) garbanzo beans
or black-eyed peas, drained and
rinsed;
or 1 1/2 cups cooked dry packaged
garbanzo beans or black-eyed peas
1 can (14 1/2 ounces) diced
 tomatoes with roasted garlic,
undrained
3/4 teaspoon dried sage leaves
1/2 teaspoon ground cumin
Salt and pepper, to taste

   1. Saute onion and green pepper in oil in large saucepan until tender, 3 to 4 minutes.
   2. Add chicken and cook over meduim heat until browned, 3 to 4 minutes.
   3. Add beans, tomatoes, and herbs to saucepan; heat to boiling. Reduce heat and simmer, uncovered, 8 to 10 minutes.
   4. Season to taste with salt and pepper.

Note: Frozen chopped onion and green pepper can be used. Stew can be prepared 1 to 2 days in advance; refrigerate, covered. Stew can also be frozen up to 2 months.

Desserts

Ruby Date Bars

Yield: 32 bars

3 cups (12 ounces) fresh or frozen cranberries, chopped
1 (8-ounce) package chopped pitted dates
1 1/2 cups water
3/4 cup granulated sugar
Grated rind of 1 lemon
1 tablespoon lemon juice
1/2 cup butter or margarine, softened
1/4 cup vegetable shortening
1 cup firmly packed brown sugar
1/2 teaspoon ground cinnamon
1/2 teaspoon salt
1/2 teaspoon baking soda
1 1/2 cups unsifted all-purpose flour
1 1/4 cups quick-cooking oats

1. In a large saucepan, place cranberries, dates, water, granulated sugar, lemon rind and juice. Bring mixture to a boil, over high heat, stirring frequently. Reduce heat; simmer, stirring occasionally, until most of liquid is evaporated, about 8 minutes. Cool thoroughly

2. Heat oven to 375 F. Grease a 13-by-9 inch baking pan.

3. In a large electric mixer bowl beat butter, shortening and brown sugar until light and fluffy. Add cinnamon, salt and baking soda. Blend in flour, about 1/2 cup at a time. Blend in oats. Mixture will look crumbly.

4. Set 2 cups of oats mixture aside for topping; press remainder evenly into pan. Spread evenly with cranberry filling; sprinkle with remaining oats mixture. Bake 25 to 27 minutes or until topping is lightly browned. Cool on wire rack. Cut into bars.

Mango-Lime Squares

Yield: 15 squares

2 cups all-purpose flour
1/2 cup confectioners' sugar
1 cup butter or margarine
2 medium-sized ripe mangoes, each
 about 3/4 pound
3 tablespoons fresh lime juice
1 tablespoon cornstarch
4 eggs
1 1/2 cups granulated sugar
Confectioners' sugar for dusting

1. In a mixing bowl, combine flour and confectioners' sugar. Cut in butter until mixture resembles coarse meal. Press mixture into a 9-by-13-inch baking pan.

2. Bake at 350 F for 25 to 30 minutes or until lightly browned. Peel, pit and dice mangoes. Place about a quarter of the diced mango in a blender or food processor; blend until smooth. Measure 1/3 cup of the pureed mixture. Add lime juice and cornstarch and blend again. Cover, refrigerate and reserve remaining mango until serving time.

3. In a large bowl, beat the eggs. Gradually add the granulated sugar, beating until thick. Stir in pureed mixture and blend well. Pour over hot crust; return to oven and bake 30 to 35 minutes until browned. Cool; cut into squares. At serving time, arrange reserved diced mango on lime squares. Dust with confectioners' sugar.

Gelatin Poke Cake

Yield: 12 to 14 servings.

1 package (2-layer size) white cake mix
or pudding-included cake mix
Oil for greasing and flour for dusting pan
1 cup boiling water
3-ounce package gelatin, any flavor
cup cold water
Whipped topping for garnish

1. Heat oven to 350 F. Prepare cake batter as directed on package and pour into well-greased and floured 13-by-9-inch pan. Bake in oven for 30 to 35 minutes until done. Cool cake in pan for 15 minutes, then prick with fork at half-inch intervals.

2. Dissolve gelatin in boiling water. Add cold water and carefully pour over cake. Chill three to four hours and garnish with whipped topping if desired.

White Diamonds

Yield: about 28 servings.

1 (6-ounce) package chopped mixed
dried fruit
1/2 cup granulated sugar
1/2 cup water
3 tablespoons safflower oil
1 1/4 cups all-purpose flour
2 egg whites
3/4 cup skim milk
1/4 cup orange juice
1 teaspoon grated orange peel
3/4 teaspoon baking soda
Confectioners' sugar (optional)

1. Heat oven to 350 F. Oil a 13-by-9 inch pan; set aside.

2. In a large saucepan, combine fruit, granulated sugar, water and safflower oil. Cook, stirring constantly, until fruit is softened, about 5 to 7 minutes. Remove pan from heat. Stir in flour, egg whites, milk, orange juice, peel and baking soda. Spread mixture in pan. Bake until wooden pick inserted in the center comes out clean, about 15 to 20 minutes.

3. Place pan on a rack to cool. When cooled completely, cut diagonally into diamond shapes. Sprinkle with confectioners' sugar. Store in an airtight container with sheets of wax paper between layers and freeze for up to 3 weeks. Bring to room temperature before serving.

S'More Bars

Yield: about 24 bars

3/4 cup (1 1/2 sticks) 70 percent
vegetable oil spread sticks
2/3 cup sugar
1 egg
1 teaspoon vanilla extract
18 whole honey-flavored or regular
 graham crackers, crushed (3 cups)
1/2 cup flour
1/2 teaspoon salt
8 chocolate bars (1.55 ounces each)
3 1/2 cups miniature marshmallows

1. Heat oven to 350 F.
2. Beat spread sticks and sugar with an
mixer on medium speed until light and fluffy.
Blend in egg and vanilla. Stir in crushed graham
crackers, flour and salt. Reserve 2 1/2 cups graham cracker mixture.

3. Press remaining mixture onto bottom of
greased 13-by-9-inch baking pan. Place chocolate
bars, side-by-side, over graham cracker mixture in
pan. Sprinkle with marshmallows. Crumble
reserved 2 1/2 cups graham cracker mixture over
marshmallows.

4. Bake 25 to 30 minutes or until golden brown.
Cool 10 minutes in pan on wire rack. Cut into
bars; cool completely.

Tropical Lime Oat Bars

Yield: 32 bars

3/4 cup sugar
1/2 cup margarine, softened
2 cups oats (quick or old-fashioned),
uncooked
1 1/4 cups all-purpose flour
1/2 teaspoon salt (optional)
1 (14-ounce) can low-fat sweetened
 condensed milk
1/2 cup low-fat sour cream
1/2 cup fresh lime juice
2 teaspoons firmly packed finely grated
 lime peel (2 to 3 limes)
1/2 cup shredded coconut
1 (3 1/2-ounce) jar macadamia nuts
 chopped (about 3/4 cup)

1. Heat oven to 350 F. Lightly grease a 13-by-9-
inch baking pan with nonstick cooking spray.

2. Beat sugar and margarine until creamy. Add
combined oats, flour and salt. Mix until crumbly.
Reserve 1 cup oat mixture for topping; set aside.
Press remaining oat mixture onto bottom of baking
pan. Bake 10 minutes.

3. Combine sweetened condensed milk, sour
cream, lime juice and lime peel; mix well. Pour
evenly over crust.

4. Combine reserved oat mixture with coconut
and nuts; mix well. Sprinkle evenly over filling.
Lightly pat topping into filling. Bake 30 minutes or
until topping is golden brown. Cool completely
before cutting.

Apricot Almond Squares

Yield: 36 squares

Butter or margarine, for greasing pan

Base:

1 package pudding-included yellow or white cake mix

1/2 cup margarine or butter, melted

1/2 cup finely chopped almonds

1 cup apricot preserves

Filling:

8 ounces cream cheese, softened

1/4 cup sugar

2 tablespoons flour

1/8 teaspoon salt

1 teaspoon vanilla extract

1 egg

1/3 cup apricot preserves

1/2 cup flaked coconut

1. Heat oven to 350 F. Generously grease a 9-by-13-inch baking pan with butter or margarine.

2. In a large bowl, combine cake mix and margarine (or butter) at low speed until crumbly. Stir in almonds. Reserve 1 cup mixture for filling. Press remaining base mixture in bottom of prepared pan. Carefully spread 1 cup preserves over base. For ease of spreading, preserves can be warmed slightly.

3. In same bowl, beat cream cheese, sugar, flour, salt, vanilla and egg until well-mixed. Blend in 1/3 cup preserves at low speed. Carefully spread filling mixture over base. Combine reserved base mixture and coconut; sprinkle over filling.

4. Bake in 350 F oven for 30 to 40 minutes or until golden brown and center is set. Cool completely. Cut into 36 squares. Store in refrigerator.

Pumpkin Pie Squares

Yield: 16-20 servings

Base:
1 cup all-purpose flour
1/2 cup quick-cooking oats
1/2 cup packed brown sugar
1/2 cup butter or margarine

Filling:
2 (15-ounce) cans pumpkin
2 (12-ounce) cans evaporated milk
4 eggs
1 1/2 cups sugar
2 teaspoons ground cinnamon
1 teaspoon ground ginger
1/2 teaspoon ground cloves
1 teaspoon salt

Topping:
1/2 cup packed brown sugar

1/2 cup chopped pecans
2 tablespoons butter or margarine, softened

1. Heat oven to 350 F. Combine the flour, quick-cooking oats, brown sugar and 1/2 cup butter or margarine. Press mixture into a greased 9-by-13 inch baking pan. Bake for 20 minutes or until golden brown.

2. Beat filling ingredients in a mixing bowl until smooth; pour over crust. Bake at 350 F for 45 minutes. Combine brown sugar, pecans and butter. Sprinkle mixture over top. Bake 15-20 minutes longer or until a knife inserted near the center comes out clean. Cool. Store in the refrigerator.

Honey Date Nut Bars

Yield: 3 round loaves

1 cup each: all-purpose flour, whole-wheat flour
1 teaspoon each: baking powder, baking soda, ground cinnamon
1/2 teaspoon salt
1 cup buttermilk
1/2 cup honey
1/4 cup vegetable oil
1 egg
1/2 cup each: pitted, chopped dates; chopped pecans

1. Heat oven to 350 F. Combine flours, baking powder, baking soda, cinnamon and salt in a large mixing bowl; set aside.

2. Beat buttermilk, honey, vegetable oil and egg until well-blended; stir into dry ingredients. Fold in dates and nuts. Pour into greased 16-ounce round tins. (Empty 16-ounce cans can be used.)

3. Bake 35 to 40 minutes or until wooden pick inserted in center comes out clean.

Mango Rum Cheesecake

Yield: 10-12 servings

Crust

1 3/4 cups graham cracker crumbs
2 ounces macadamia nuts
1/2 teaspoon ground ginger
1/3 cup butter, melted

1. To make the crust, in a work bowl of a food processor fitted with a metal blade, place the graham cracker crumbs, nuts and ginger. Process until finely ground. Pour in melted butter and pulse until evenly moistened. Transfer mixture to a 10-inch springform pan and press the crust evenly over the bottom and halfway up the sides of the pan. Place in freezer while preparing filling.

Filling

1 pound cream cheese
1 cup sugar
3 eggs
1 cup mango pieces
1/3 cup Barcardi Gold rum
1 teaspoon grated zest of lemon
3 cups sour cream

2. Heat oven to 375F. Place all ingredients except sour cream in the work bowl of a food processor. Process 10-20 seconds, until smooth. Add sour cream and pulse briefly to blend. Pour mixture into the prepared crust and bake 30-35 minutes. The center will appear very loose and the top will probably not be brown. Turn the oven off and leave the cheesecake in the oven, with the door closed, for 15 minutes. Remove cheesecake from oven and let cool on a wire rack. Place cooled cheesecake in the refrigerator overnight.

Topping

2 cups diced mango
1/2 sugar
3 tablespoons Barcardi Gold rum
1 teaspoon grated zest of lemon

3. To make topping, put all ingredients in a saucepan over medium heat. Bring to a boil, stirring frequently. Lower heat and simmer 10-12 minutes, until thickened slightly. Cool and refrigerate overnight.

4. Remove cheesecake from refrigerator and remove sides from springform pan. Place cheesecake on a serving platter and spread the mango topping over the top. Slice and serve.

Blueberry Coffeecake

Blueberry Coffeecake

Yield: 9 servings

3/4 cup sugar
1/4 cup butter or margarine
2 eggs
1 teaspoon vanilla extract
2 cups flour
2 teaspoons baking powder
1/2 teaspoon salt
1/2 cup buttermilk
2 1/2 cups fresh or frozen blueberries

1. Heat oven to 375F. Blend sugar and butter until creamy in texture. Beat in eggs and vanilla.

2. Combine flour, baking powder and salt. Add flour mixture and buttermilk alternately to batter. Stir in berries. Spread batter in a lightly greased 9-inch square baking pan.

3. Combine topping ingredients and sprinkle over batter in pan. Bake 25-30 minutes or until a wooden pick inserted near the center comes out clean.

Topping
1/4 cup sugar
1/4 cup packed brown sugar
1/4 cup flour
1/4 cup butter or margarine
1/2 teaspoon ground cinnamon

Blueberry Tips

● How to store: Blueberries keep longer than any other berry when refrigerated (from 10 days to 2 weeks). Put clean, store-bought berries in refrigerator in bowl for quick snacks or desserts. Berries are more perishable at room temperature.

● How to freeze: Wash berries and dry thoroughly before putting the fruit in freezer containers. Dry blueberries will pour freely like marbles when frozen and won't stick together. Wet berries will freeze in a clump.

● How to prepare: This fruit is nature's convenience food. They need no peeling, coring or pitting. Only washing is required.

● How to buy: Look for berries that are plump and full with a light, powdery, gray-blue color.

Black Walnut Cake

Black Walnut Cake

Yield: 10 to 12 servings

1/2 cup butter, softened
1/2 cup solid shortening
2 cups sugar
5 eggs, separated
1 cup buttermilk
1 teaspoon baking soda
2 cups all-purpose flour
1 teaspoon vanilla
1 1/2 cups black walnuts (regular walnuts can be substituted)
1 (3-ounce) can flaked coconut
1/2 teaspoon cream of tartar

1. Heat oven to 350F. Blend butter and solid shortening until creamy in texture. Gradually add sugar, beating until light and fluffy and sugar is dissolved. Add egg yolks and beat well.

2. Combine buttermilk and baking soda, stirring until soda is dissolved.

3. Add flour to butter mixture alternately with buttermilk mixture, ending with flour. Add vanilla, walnuts and coconut, stir thoroughly.

4. Beat 5 egg whites with cream of tartar until stiff peaks form. Fold egg whites into batter. Pour batter into 3 greased and floured 9-inch cake pans. Bake for 30 minutes, or until cake tests done. Cool in pans for 10 minutes, then remove from pans to finish cooling.

Butter Cream Frosting

6 to 8 egg whites
12 ounces sugar
1 cup water
1 pound butter
3 ounces black walnuts (regular walnuts can be substituted)

1. To make frosting, whip 6 to 8 egg whites until frothy. Combine sugar and 1 cup water and heat to 240 F (use a candy thermometer). Slowly pour sugar mixture into egg whites while beating. Whip until cooled. Add butter in chunks until butter is completely incorporated. Fold in walnuts.

2. Frost cake layers with icing and serve.

Chocolate Macaroon Squares

Yield: About 2 dozen squares

1 (18 1/4 -ounce) box chocolate cake mix
1/3 cup butter or margarine, softened
2 eggs
1 (14-ounce) can sweetened condensed milk (1 1/4 cups), not evaporated milk
1 teaspoon vanilla extract
2 cups (12-ounce package) semi-sweet chocolate chips
1 1/3 cups flaked coconut
3/4 cup chopped nuts (optional)

1. Beat the cake mix, butter and 1 egg in a large mixer bowl until mixture is crumbly. Firmly press onto bottom of greased 9-by-13-inch baking pan.

2. Combine sweetened condensed milk, remaining egg and vanilla in medium pan and stir in chocolate chips, 1 cup of the coconut and the nuts, if using.

Spread over crust. Sprinkle with remaining coconut.

3. Bake in a 350 F oven for 30 to 40 minutes or until golden brown (center will set when cooled).

4. Cool in pan on wire rack.

Chocolate Chip Cookies

Yield: about 112 cookies

5 cups blended oatmeal
2 cups butter
2 cups sugar
2 cups brown sugar
4 eggs
2 teaspoons vanilla
4 cups flour
1 teaspoon salt
2 teaspoons baking powder
2 teaspoons baking soda
24 ounces chocolate chips
1 (8-ounce) Hershey Bar, grated
3 cups chopped nuts (optional)

1. Heat oven to 375 F.

2. Measure oatmeal and process in a blender to a powder. Cream butter and sugars. Add eggs and vanilla. Mix together with flour, blended oatmeal, salt, baking powder and soda. Add chips, grated chocolate and nuts.

3. Roll into balls. Place 2 inches apart on a cookie sheet. Bake 10 minutes.

Homemade ice cream sandwiches

Marco Island Peanut Butter Pie

Yield: 8 to 10 servings

1 cup confectioners' sugar
1 cup cream cheese
1 1/2 cups smooth peanut butter
4 ounces (1/2 cup) heavy cream
1 cup sweetened whipped cream or
whipped topping
Chocolate curls and crushed peanuts for
garnish (optional)
Pie crust:
12 Oreo cookies, crushed
1 1/2 tablespoons melted butter or
margarine

1. To make pie crust, mix cookies and melted butter. Press mixture into 9-inch pie pan. Bake in 350 F oven for 5 minutes. Allow to cool before filling.

2. Blend confectioners' sugar and cream cheese until smooth. Add peanut butter and blend until smooth. Slowly add heavy cream. Fold in whipped cream, reserving some to use as a garnish.

3. Pour into cooled pie shell and chill until set. Mound extra whipped cream on top and garnish with crushed peanuts and/or chocolate curls and chill again. Serve well-chilled.

Quick Summer desserts

1. Make ice cream sandwiches with oversized cookies and slightly softened ice cream or frozen yogurt.

2. Create shortcakes by halving baked Pillsbury Grand Biscuits and topping with low-fat whipped cream and strawberry slices.

3. Construct elegant little Napoleons by layering chocolate wafers, fudge sauce, dollops of ready-to-serve custard, sliced strawberries and shredded mint.

4. Buy a plain sheet-cake covered with white icing and turn dessert into a party game for the kids. Give them each a tube of icing and let them decorate the cake. Be sure to get a photo of the cake artists with their artwork before you cut the cake.

5. Drizzle almond liqueur on chocolate brownies, top with whipped cream and a carambola slice and garnish with slivered almonds.

6. Ladle berries that have been soaked in spiced rum over frozen yogurt or ice cream.

7. Lighten old-fashioned root beer floats with low-fat frozen yogurt.

8. Let guests serve themselves from a pot of chocolate fondue on a warm grill. Have the usual dunkers ready: cubed angel food cake, banana slices, dried apricots and, of course, strawberries.

Strawberry Shortbread Shortcake

8 servings

1 cup butter or margarine, softened
1 cup powdered sugar
2 cups flour
1 ounce grated semisweet chocolate
(about 1/3 cup)

1 cup whipping cream, whipped and sweetened
2 pints fresh strawberries, sliced
Whole fresh strawberry, for garnish

1. Heat oven to 350 F.
2. In mixer bowl, blend butter and sugar. On low speed gradually mix in flour and chocolate.

3. Form dough into 2 balls, one a little larger than the other. On floured surface roll each ball to a circle about 7 inches in diameter (one should be thicker than the other).

4. Using broad spatula, gently transfer each circle to greased baking sheet. Prick surfaces generously with a fork.

5. Bake for 20 to 30 minutes until just golden. While still warm, cut thinner circle into 8 equal wedges. Transfer both to a rack to cool completely.

6. To serve, place shortbread circle on serving plate. Top with whipped cream and sliced strawberries, reserving a dollop of cream for garnish. Set shortbread wedges into cream at an angle, points toward center. Top with a dollop of whipped cream and whole strawberry. Cut into wedges.

Note: Shortbread can be made ahead and stored for several days wrapped in plastic wrap, or frozen for longer storage.

96

Classic 7-Up Poundcake

Yield: 1 10-inch pouncake, 12 to 16 servings.

2 sticks unsalted butter, softened
1/2 cup solid vegetable shortening
3 1/2 cups sugar
1 teaspoon vanilla extract
1 teaspoon almond extract
1 teaspoon butter-flavored extract
5 large eggs
3 cups all-purpose flour
1/2 teaspoon salt
1 1/4 cups 7 Up

1. Grease and flour a 10-inch tube pan. Heat oven to 300 F.
2. Combine and beat the butter, shortening, 3 cups of the sugar, vanilla, almond and butter-flavored extracts in a large mixing bowl, at high speed, until light and fluffy.

Add the eggs, one at a time, beating well after each addition.

3. Stir together the flour and salt. Alternately add the flour and 1 cup of the 7 Up to the butter-sugar mixture, beating well after each addition. Spoon batter to the prepared tube pan. Bake at 300 F for 1 3/4 to 2 hours or until a tester comes out clean. Let cool in pan on a wire rack for 10 minutes.

4. If necessary, run a knife around the inside edge of pan to loosen cake. Invert onto rack or platter. Meanwhile, combine the remaining 1/2 cup sugar and 1/4 cup 7 Up in a small saucepan and bring to a boil. Boil for 2 to 3 minutes or until sugar dissolves. With a toothpick or skewer, pierce holes over the top of the cake. Spoon the hot glaze over the cake. Let cool completely.

The Commander's Cherry Bars

Yield: about 24 servings

1 cup butter or margarine
1 1/4 cups sugar
1 egg
1 teaspoon vanilla
2 1/2 cups flour
1/2 teaspoon salt
1 1/2 teaspoons baking powder
1/2 cup chopped nuts
1/2 cup maraschino cherries, chopped
2/3 cup flaked coconut
6 ounces chocolate chips

1. Cream the butter and then add the sugar gradually.
2. Blend in the egg and the vanilla. Sift the dry ingredients together and stir into the creamed mixture. Add remaining ingredients.
3. Spread dough in greased 9-by-13-inch baking pan. Bake at 375 F for about 25 minutes or until firm in center. Cool slightly and then cut into bars.

Chocolate Chip Cookie Bars

Chocolate Chip Cookie Bars

Yield: 48 bars

2 1/4 cups all-purpose flour
1/3 cup cocoa
1 teaspoon baking soda
1/2 teaspoon salt
1 cup (2 sticks) butter, softened
3/4 cup granulated sugar
3/4 cup packed light brown sugar
1 teaspoon vanilla extract
2 eggs
2 cups semisweet chocolate chips
1 cup chopped nuts (optional)

1. Heat oven to 375 F. Stir together flour, cocoa, baking soda and salt.

2. In a large bowl, beat butter, granulated sugar, brown sugar and vanilla on medium speed of electric mixer until creamy. Add eggs; beat well. Gradually add flour mixture, beating well. Stir in chocolate chips and nuts, if using.

3. Spread batter evenly in greased 15 1/2 -by-10 1/2 -by-1-inch jellyroll pan. Bake 20 - 22 minutes or until cookies begin to pull away from sides of pan.

Lemon Bars

Yield: 36 bars.

4 eggs
1 cup granulated sugar
1 teaspoon vanilla
1/4 cup vegetable oil
3 teaspoons grated lemon peel
2 tablespoons lemon juice
3/4 cup all-purpose flour
2/3 cup chopped walnuts
2 tablespoons powdered sugar

1. In large bowl of an electric mixer, beat eggs and granulated sugar on high speed until about tripled in volume (about 5 minutes.) Beat in vanilla, oil, 1 teaspoon of the lemon peel, lemon juice and flour. Stir in walnuts.

2. Pour batter into a buttered, flour-dusted 7-by-11-inch baking pan. Bake on the center rack of a 375 F oven until cake begins to pull from pan sides and center feels set when lightly pressed (about 25 minutes). Let cake cool completely in pan on a rack. If made ahead, cover and let stand at room temperature until next day.

3. To serve, sift powdered sugar over top of cake and cut into rectangles about 1-by-2 inches. Garnish rectangles with remaining 2 teaspoons lemon peel.

Scrumptious Chocolate Peanut Butter Cake

This is delicious party dessert that's perfect for a festive picnic.
Yield: 15 servings

2 cups all-purpose flour
1 1/2 cups sugar
1/2 cup unsweetened cocoa
1/2 cup Land o' Lakes butter, softened
1 cup water
3 eggs
1 1/4 teaspoons baking powder
1 teaspoon baking soda
1 teaspoon vanilla
1 cup miniature semisweet chocolate chips

Frosting
2/3 cup Land O' Lakes butter, softened
1/3 cup peanut butter
4 cups powdered sugar
4 to 5 tablespoons half-and-half or milk
1 cup miniature semisweet chocolate chips
1/2 cup chopped salted peanuts

1. Heat oven to 350 F.

2. In large mixer bowl, combine all cake ingredients except chocolate chips. Beat at low speed, scraping bowl often, until moistened.

3. Beat at high speed, scraping bowl often, until well-mixed, 1-2 minutes. By hand, stir in the 1 cup chocolate chips. Pour into greased and floured 9-by-13-inch baking pan. Bake in a 350 F oven for 30-40 minutes or until wooden pick inserted in center comes out clean. Cool completely.

4. For the frosting, in medium bowl, combine the 2/3 cup butter and the 1/3 cup peanut butter. Beat at high speed, scraping bowl often, until light and creamy, 1-2 minutes. Reduce speed to low; add powdered sugar. Beat, gradually adding half-and-half and scraping bowl often, until smooth, 1-2 minutes. Frost cooled cake; sprinkle with the 1 cup chocolate chips and the salted peanuts.

Star-Studded Fruit Basket

*For this elegant dessert, a watermelon is carved in the shape of a basket
and filled with assorted fresh fruit. Serve the fruit with honey-poppy seed dressing.
Yield: 1 basket, 1 cup dressing*

Dressing

1/4 cup honey
1/4 cup frozen orange juice
concentrate, thawed
1/2 cup whipping cream
1 teaspoon poppy seeds
1/4 teaspoon ginger

Basket:

Large watermelon
Assorted fresh fruits

1. In a small bowl stir together honey
and orange juice concentrate. Stir all
remaining dressing ingredients into the
honey-orange mixture. Cover; refrigerate 1
hour.

2. To make the watermelon basket, measure and mark a horizontal line around the
center of the melon, running lengthwise.
Measure and mark a 2-inch wide center
strip crosswise over the top of the melon for
the handle.   Place 1 1/2 -inch star-
shaped cookie cutter or cardboard pattern
on marked horizontal line; trace around
with pencil.

Repeat, with star tips touching, all
around middle of melon. Place star shape
in center of 2-inch handle strip; trace
around with pencil. Repeat, with star tips
touching, over handle. With a small sharp
knife cut out stars, leaving bottom points
attached to watermelon. Remove rind and
melon. Cut out stars on handle, leaving

bottom and top tips attached to one another.
Carefully cut pink melon from handle, leaving white
rind on handle.

3. Remove remaining watermelon from basket
with melon baller or spoon. Fill basket with assorted fresh fruit pieces. Serve dressing with fresh fruit.

*Note: Melon basket can be prepared one day
ahead. Wrap tightly in plastic wrap and refrigerate. Just before serving, fill with assorted fresh fruit
pieces.*

Edwina Gadsby's Brownie Souffle Cake With Mint Creme

Yield: 12 servings

2/3 cup whipping cream
3 ounces white chocolate baking bar,
finely chopped
1/4 to 1/2 teaspoon mint extract
Cake:
1 (1-pound, 5.5-ounce) package
Pillsbury Rich & Moist Fudge Brownie
Mix
1/2 cup water
1/2 cup oil
1/2 to 1 teaspoon mint extract (optional)
4 eggs, separated
Powdered sugar
Mint sprigs (optional)

1. Heat oven to 350 F. Spray a 9- or 10-inch springform pan with nonstick cooking spray. In a medium size, microwave-safe bowl, microwave whipping cream on high (100 percent) power for 45 to 60 seconds or until warm. Add white chocolate and 1/4 to 1/2 teaspoon mint extract. Stir until chocolate is melted. Refrigerate at least 1 hour or until well-chilled.

2. In a large bowl, combine brownie mix, water, oil, 1/2 to 1 teaspoon mint extract and egg yolks; beat 50 strokes with a spoon. In a small bowl, beat egg whites until soft peaks form. Gradually fold into brownie mixture. Pour batter into sprayed pan.

3. Bake for 32 to 38 minutes or until the center is almost set. Cool for 30 minutes. The center will sink slightly. Carefully remove the sides of the pan. Sprinkle top of the cake with powdered sugar.

4. Just before serving, combine ingredients for mint cream. Beat until soft peaks form. Cut cake into wedges. Top each wedge with mint cream. Garnish with mint sprigs.

Note: This recipe made Gadsby a finalist in the 38th Pillsbury Bake-Off Contest.

Meadow Marsh's Chocolate Walnut Pie

Meadow Marsh is a lovely bed and breakfast in Orange County, Florida.
Yield: 2 (9-inch) pies

2 pie shells, baked 10 minutes
12-ounce package chocolate chips
1 1/2 cups chopped English walnuts
1 stick butter, melted in double boiler
1 cup sugar
1 cup white Karo syrup
4 eggs, beaten
4 tablespoons bourbon

1. Heat oven to 350 F. In bottom of each baked pie shell sprinkle half a 12-ounce package chocolate chips and 3/4 cup chopped English walnuts.

2. Combine butter, sugar, Karo syrup, eggs and bourbon. Divide mixture among the pie shells.

3. Bake for 10 minutes. Turn oven to 325 F and bake 30-35 more minutes or until center does not move and knife comes out clean. Let cool at room temperature.

Betty Boza's Guava Bread Pudding

Yield: depending on appetites, can serve up to 30 people.

3/4 loaf day-old Cuban bread
4 eggs, beaten
1 large can evaporated milk
1 can condensed milk
1 cup sugar
1 teaspoon vanilla
1 stick margarine
1 small box of guava paste

1. Break the bread into pieces and soak in water to cover for about 5 to 10 minutes. Drain bread pieces thoroughly in a colander.

2. Place the bread in a large bowl. Add eggs, evaporated and condensed milks, sugar and vanilla. Melt the butter in a 9-by-13-inch baking pan. Pour melted butter into egg mixture. Mix ingredients throughly and pour the mixture back into the baking pan.

3. Cut the guava paste into small strips. Insert into bread mixture in rows. Bake at 350 F for 1 hour. Cool.

Honey Blondies

Honey Blondies

Yield: 16 squares

1 cup honey
3/4 cup butter or margarine, softened
1 egg
1 teaspoon vanilla extract
2 cups all-purpose flour
1/2 teaspoon baking powder
1/2 cup semi-sweet chocolate chips
1/2 cup chopped toasted pecans

1. Heat oven to 350F.

2. In a medium-size bowl, blend honey and butter until light and fluffy. Beat in egg and vanilla. Add flour and baking powder. Mix until well-blended. Fold in chocolate chips and pecans.

3. Spread batter into a greased 9-by-9-inch square baking dish for 40 minutes, or until a wooden pick inserted near the center comes out clean. Cool completely. Cut into squares.

Lemon Butter Poundcake Bars

Yield: 48 bars

1 cup butter or margarine
2 cups sugar
4 eggs
2 cups self-rising flour
1/3 cup fresh lemon juice
2 tablespoons grated lemon peel
Lemon glaze:
1 cup powdered sugar
2 tablespoons lemon juice

1. Heat oven to 375F. Grease bottom of 9-by-13-inch pan.

2. In large saucepan, melt butter over medium heat, remove from heat. Stir sugar, eggs, flour, 1/3 cup lemon juice and grated peel, mixing well after each addition.

3. Spread batter in prepared pan. Bake for 35-45 minutes or until top is golden brown. Cool 10 minutes.

4. To make glaze, combine powdered sugar with remaining lemon juice. Drizzle over cooled bars.

Devon Delaney's Chewy Cinnamon Trail Bars

Yield: 24 bars

1 cup old-fashioned or quick-cooking rolled oats
1/2 cup firmly-packed brown sugar
1/3 cup coconut
1/3 cup white vanilla chips
1/3 cup pecan pieces
1 package Pillsbury Cinnamon Swirl Quick bread mix
1/2 cup butter or margarine, melted
1/3 cup water
2 egg yolks

1. Heat oven to 375 F. Grease a 12-by-8-inch (2 quart) baking dish or a 9-by-13-inch pan.

2. In a food processor fitted with a metal blade, combine oats, brown sugar, coconut, vanilla chips and pecans. Process 10 seconds or until coarsely ground.

3. Set cinnamon swirl package from the Pillsbury bread mix aside. In a large bowl, combine remaining bread mix from package and oat mixture. Stir in the butter, water and egg yolks and mix well. Spread half of the batter into a prepared pan. Sprinkle batter in pan with the contents of the cinnamon swirl package. Drop remaining batter by spoonfuls over the cinnamon swirl mix. Carefully spread the dollops of batter over top.

4. Bake for 25 to 30 minutes or until the edges are firm. Cool until completely cooled, about 2 hours. Cut into bars.

Note: This recipe made Delaney a finalist in the 38th Pillsbury Bake-Off Contest.

Big Dipper Oatmeal Cookies

Yield: About 4 dozen cookies

1 cup butter or margarine, softened
1 cup firmly packed brown sugar
1/2 cup granulated sugar
2 eggs
1 teaspoon vanilla
1 1/2 cups all-purpose flour
1 teaspoon baking soda
1 teaspoon ground cinnamon
1/2 teaspoon salt (optional)
3 cups oats (quick or old-fashioned, uncooked)
1 cup raisins or semisweet chocolate pieces (optional)

Glaze
2 cups semisweet chocolate pieces
3/4 cup chopped nuts

1. Heat oven to 350 F. Beat butter and sugars until creamy. Add eggs and vanilla; beat well. Add combined flour, baking soda, cinnamon and salt; mix well. Stir in oats and, if desired, raisins or chocolate pieces; mix well.

2. Drop dough by rounded tablespoonfuls onto ungreased cookie sheet.

3. Bake 10-12 minutes or until light golden brown. Cool 1 minute on cookie sheets; remove to wire rack. Cool completely.

4. Melt chocolate pieces according to package directions. Dip half of one cookie in chocolate; gently shake to remove excess. Sprinkle with chopped nuts. Place on waxed paper until set. Repeat with remaining cookies. If chocolate thickens, microwave at 15-second intervals until fluid.

5. Store cookies with wax paper between layers in tightly covered container.

107

Country-Style Apple Pie

Yield: 6 servings

1 (15-ounce) package Pillsbury Refrigerated Pie Crusts
1/2 cup sugar
4 teaspoons cornstarch
2 teaspoons cinnamon
4 cups thinly sliced peeled apples
1 teaspoon sugar
2 tablespoons chopped pecans

1. Heat oven to 450 F. Combine 1/2 cup sugar, cornstarch, and cinnamon; mix well. Add apples and toss gently.

2. Place one pie crust on large cookie sheet (refreeze the other crust for another use). Spoon apple mixture on center of crust to within 2 inches from edge. Fold unfilled sides of crust over apple mixture; crimp slightly. Brush crust edge with water; sprinkle with 1 teaspoon sugar.

3. Bake for 15 minutes or until golden brown. Sprinkle pecans over apple mixture. Bake for an additional 10-15 minutes or until apples are tender.

Coffee Ice-Cream Pie

Yield: 8 to 10 servings

Crust

20 Oreo cookies
5 1/3 tablespoons unsalted butter, melted

Sauce

2 ounces unsweetened chocolate
1/2 cup sugar
1 tablespoon unsalted butter
2/3 cup evaporated milk
2 pints coffee-flavored ice cream, softened
1 cup heavy whipping cream
2 tablespoons coffee liqueur

1. Crush cookies in a food processor or blender. Process until they develop a fine crumb consistency.

Add melted butter and mix well. Press the mixture into the bottom of a 10-inch pie pan and freeze.

2. Combine unsweetened chocolate, sugar, butter and milk in the top of a double boiler. Cook, stirring, over boiling water until the sauce thickens up a bit. Cool mixture.

3. Spread ice cream into prepared crust. Freeze until firm.

4. Whip heavy whipping cream and liqueur until stiff, but not dry.

5. Pour the cooled chocolate sauce evenly over the ice cream, then spread whipped cream topping over the chocolate sauce. Cover with plastic wrap and freeze for at least four hours or overnight. Remove pie from freezer 20 minutes before serving.

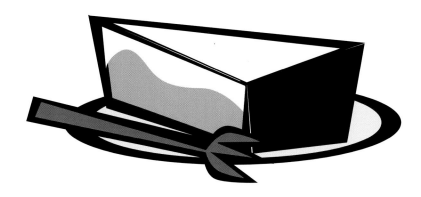

Chocolate Chip Pear Bars

Yield: 24 servings

1 (16-ounce) can pear halves or slices, drained
1/2 cup butter or margarine, softened
1 cup packed brown sugar
4 large egg whites
2 teaspoons vanilla extract
2 cups quick-cooking rolled oats
1 1/2 cups all-purpose flour
1/2 teaspoon baking soda
1/4 teaspoon salt
2/3 cup semi-sweet chocolate chips

1. Heat oven to 350 F. Grease a 9-by-13-inch baking pan. Dice pears and set aside.

2. In medium bowl, cream together butter and brown sugar until light and fluffy. Blend in egg whites, vanilla and pears.

3. In separate bowl, combine oats, flour, baking soda and salt. Stir dry ingredients into pear mixture; mix well. Stir in chocolate chips.

4. Spread batter in prepared baking pan. Bake for 25-30 minutes or until golden brown on top. Cool on rack and cut into squares.

Nikki Norman's Zesty Key Lime Pie

Yield: 8 servings

2 cups finely crushed vanilla wafer crumbs
1/4 cup packed light brown sugar
1/2 teaspoon grated nutmeg
1 1/2 sticks unsalted butter (1 stick melted, 1/2 reserved)
1 can (14-ounce) condensed milk
1 package (8-ounce) cream cheese, softened
3/4 cup freshly squeezed Key lime juice
1/2 teaspoon vanilla

Topping:
6 ounces white chocolate, chopped
4 tablespoons unsalted butter
2 cups heavy whipping cream
2 ounces macadamia nuts, chopped
1 Key lime, thinly sliced for garnish

1. Heat oven to 400 F. In a medium mixing bowl combine the vanilla wafer crumbs, brown sugar, nutmeg and melted butter. Pat mixture evenly onto bottom and sides of a deep-dish 9-inch greased pie pan. Bake for 8 minutes or until lightly browned. Cool.

2. In a blender combine the condensed milk, cream cheese and Key lime juice. Blend on low speed until smooth. Add vanilla. Pour into pre-baked nutmeg crust.

Topping
1. Melt white chocolate and butter in a double boiler. Allow mixture to cool.

2. Beat cream until stiff. Fold into cooled chocolate. Fold in macadamia nuts.

3. Spread topping on pie. Refrigerate at least 4 hours before serving. Garnish with lime slices.

Watermelon Slice Dessert

Yield: 12 servings

1 quart lime sherbet
1 quart vanilla ice cream
Miniature chocolate chips
Store-bought or homemade watermelon sorbet

1. To make the watermelon sorbet, puree about 3 pounds of seeded watermelon cubes. Strain mixture. Transfer half the mixture to a saucepan and add 1 cup sugar. Stir and bring to a boil, stirring often, until sugar has dissolved. Remove from heat. Stir in 3 tablespoons fresh lemon juice, a few drops of red food coloring (or more to achieve desired color), 2 tablespoons raspberry vinegar, a splash of almond extract and remaining watermelon juice. Freeze overnight. When ready to prepare dessert, process in small batches in a food processor or blender until sorbet consistency is reached.

2. Press spoonfuls of lime sherbet along the inside wall of a 9-inch springform pan. Spread evenly to form a 2 inch layer. Center of pan will remain empty. Cover pan with plastic wrap and freeze until firm, about 1 hour.

3. Spoon vanilla ice cream in an even layer up against the lime sherbet. Re-cover pan and freeze until firm, about 1 hour.

4. Spoon frozen watermelon sorbet into center of springform pan, packing sorbet to remove air holes. Smooth top of watermelom sorbet so that it is level with the green and white borders. Freeze any leftover watermelon sorbet for another use.

5. Decorate with chocolate chip "seeds." Cover and freeze overnight.

6. Carefully remove sides of springform pan. Slice into wedges and serve immediately.

Luscious Libations

Apple Iced Tea

Yield: 1 serving

5 ounces apple juice
3 ounces canned iced tea without lemon
1 ounce fresh lemon juice
3 ounces ice
1 lemon slice for garnish

1. Combine the apple juice, tea and lemon juice in a 12-ounce glass. Stir, then add ice. Garnish with the lemon slice.

Strawberry Tea Fizz

Yield: 12 servings

1 pint strawberries, stemmed and sliced
1/2 cup sugar
5 cups boiling water
1 orange pekoe tea bag
1 (12-ounce) can frozen lemonade concentrate, thawed
1 quart chilled sparkling water
Ice cubes

1. In a large bowl, combine strawberries and sugar and set aside.
2. In another bowl, pour water over tea bag and steep 5 minutes. Discard tea bag and cool tea to room temperature. Stir tea into strawberry mixture along with lemonade concentrate and chill. To serve, stir in sparkling water and ladle over ice cubes in tall glasses. Serve with spoons.

Peach Iced Tea

Yield: 4 servings

4 regular tea bags
3 teaspoons peach (or other fruit) flavoring
Sugar to taste

1. Brew tea. Let cool.
2. Add flavoring. Add ice to serve. Sweeten to taste.

Herbal Iced Tea

Yield: 4 servings

1 gallon filtered water
3 flavored herbal tea bags (peppermint, strawberry, lemon)
Sugar to taste

1. Place tea bags in water. Let steep overnight.
2. Add ice to serve. Sweeten to taste.

Watermelon Daiquiri

Yield: 1 serving

2 cups seeded watermelon pulp
1/2 cup light rum
2 tablespoons fresh lime juice
2 tablespoons orange-flavored liqueur
5 to 6 ice cubes
Skewered watermelon for garnish

1. Freeze watermelon cubes in shallow pan 6 hours or longer. Puree watermelon with rum, lime juice and liqueur in blender until smooth. Add ice cubes, one at a time, and blend until smooth.

2. Pour into large, stemmed glass and decorate with skewered watermelon and a straw.

Strawberry Colada Float

Yield: 4 servings

1 pint strawberries
1/3 cup coconut cream
1/3 cup light rum
2 1/2 cups crushed ice
4 orange slices

1. Reserve 4 whole berries for garnish, set aside. Hull and slice remaining berries (makes about 1 3/4 cups). Place berries in a blender. Blend until smooth, stopping occasionally to scrape down the sides of containers.

2. Add coconut cream, rum and crushed ice. Blend until smooth.

3. Pour into tall glasses. Garnish each glass with a reserved whole berry and an orange slice.

Strawberry Sangria Ice

Strawberry Sangria Ice

Yield: 4 servings

2 pints fresh strawberries, stemmed and
 divided
1/4 cup sugar
1 cup dry red wine
2 tablespoons lemon juice
1 1/2 tablespoons frozen orange juice
concentrate, thawed
Sparkling water
Orange slices
Mint sprigs for garnish

1. In a large bowl, crush 1/2 pint of the strawberries with the sugar. Add wine, lemon juice and orange juice concentrate. Stir to dissolve sugar. Pour into a shallow pan and freeze until firm 1 to 2 inches around the rim. Stir to blend and freeze again until firm.

2. To serve, fill 4 stemmed glasses with spoonfuls of the sangria ice and the remaining strawberries, halved. Reserve four whole strawberries for garnish.) Fill with sparkling water. Garnish with strawberries, orange slices and mint sprigs. Serve with spoons and straws.

Watermelon Strawberry Shake

Yield : 4 servings

1 (8-ounce) container lemon nonfat yogurt
2 cups cubed seeded watermelon
1 pint fresh strawberries
1 medium banana, peeled and sliced

1. In a blender or food processor, combine yogurt, watermelon, strawberries and banana until smooth and frothy. Serve immediately.

Banana Lemonade Cooler

Yield: 1 serving

1 large banana
1/4 cup fresh lemon juice
2 tablespoons water
4 teaspoons honey
6 ice cubes
2 small mint leaves
Lemon slice for garnish

1. In a blender, combine banana, juice, water, honey, ice and mint leaves. Blend until smooth.

2. Pour over ice cubes in a tall glass. Garnish with lemon.

Honey Mint Juleps

Honey Mint Juleps

Yield: 14 servings

1 cup water
1 1/2 cups mint leaves
1 cup honey
3 1/2 cups bourbon
Crushed ice
Mint sprigs for garnish

1. In a small saucepan, bring water to a boil. Remove from heat. Add mint leaves and stir until wilted. Add 1 cup honey. Stir until dissolved. Let mixture stand until cool. Strain mixture and discard mint.

2. For each julep, combine 1/4 cup bourbon with 2 tablespoons of the honey mint syrup. Pour bourbon mixture over crushed ice in frosted tumbler or tall glass. Garnish with mint sprig.

Golden Blossom Honey Lemonade

Yield: 5 cups

4 lemons
1 orange
1 lime
1 cup warm water
3 cups cold water
1/2 cup honey
Lemon slices for garnish
Strawberries for garnish

1. Squeeze juice from fruit into a pitcher.

2. Mix honey with warm water and add to pitcher along with 3 cups of cold water. Stir in a dozen ice cubes.

3. Garnish with lemon slices, strawberries, sprigs of mint.

Watermelon Vase

Entertaining Tips

Let there be light

Set the mood for outdoor evening parties by covering a glass-topped patio table with a lace tablecloth and placing a spotlight shining upward under the table.

Appetite teaser

Create a mouth-watering aroma by rubbing an onion across the grill before you light the barbecue.

Welcome to water world

If the barbecue party theme includes fish and shellfish on the menu, consider these entertaining ideas:

● Go fishing for beverages: Use a fun, fish-shaped tureen as a vessel for fruity sangria or a light, white wine punch.

● Nothing but net: Lay inexpensive mock fisherman's net over outdoor serving tables to set a seaside tone. (These are usually sold at party stores in packages with assorted decorative shells.)

Stir and serve dips

Start with 2 cups light sour cream and add an envelope of one of the following dry seasoning mixes:

- ● Blue cheese dressing.
- ● Caesar dressing.
- ● Cheese garlic dressing.
- ● Italian dressing.
- ● Onion soup or dip.
- ● Sesame dressing.
- ● Parmesan dressing.
- ● Ranch dip or dressing.
- ● Vegetable soup.
- ● Zesty herb dressing.

How to make a watermelon vase

This is a beautiful centerpiece for outdoor parties.
It only takes about 15 minutes to make this spectacular table ornament.

1. Select a symmetrical oblong watermelon.
2. Measure 9 inches from one end of watermelon. Cut crosswise for vase.
3. Reserve shorter section for your favorite watermelon recipe.
4. Cut a thick slice from end of watermelon vase so it sits upright.
5. Remove about 1-inch layer of flesh from top of watermelon vase to form rim.
6. Place watermelon vase on small, sturdy plate to protect table surface.
7. Arrange your choice of flowers and greenery in watermelon vase.

The watermelon flesh will hold the flowers in place and provide moisture.

Parsley Plant Centerpiece

Parsley's dark green leaves are one of the most popular garnishes used in the kitchen. Too bad the herb often hovers alone on the edge of the plate long after the meal has been consumed. It's often used only to add a bright dash of color to the day's meal.

Consider a potted parsley plant or a flower vase filled with the fresh herb to add a burst of green on the table as a centerpiece.

Parsley is abundant and inexpensive in the grocery store all year. Look for tightly bunched leaves with no signs of wilting or browning. The leaves should look moist and smell very aromatic.

Store the fresh parsley upright in a jar of water, or wash leaves in cool water and seal them in a plastic bag. With both methods, store the parsley in the refrigerator for up to two weeks. Potted parsley plants are sold in full-service garden shops and some supermarkets.

And in the garden don't think of parsley as merely a kitchen herb. Compact curly varieties are wonderful in borders and flower beds as a green backdrop for more colorful flowers. Italian types, which often grow to 3 feet, can be used at the back of a flower bed.

Running out of serving pieces?

Serve poached dessert fruits in clear tumblers instead of in small bowls or on standard dessert plates. The see-through vessels will showcase the colorful fruit and create an interesting presentation.

Also, slender glasses, such as acrylic sparkling wine flutes can hold biscotti, chocolate-dipped pretzel sticks, shortbread wedges and rolled cookies.

index